Splendid & Permanent P

Archaeological & historical reconstruction pictures of Essex

compiled by Nigel Brown

Foreword

by Councillor Joan Lyon

The publication of this colourful book of historical and archaeological reconstruction pictures is part of Essex County Council's celebration of the millennium. The book displays the extraordinary variety of the County's heritage. Since its creation more than a hundred years ago the County Council has been keenly aware of the importance of Essex's past. The County has an immense history.

Having been a recognisable entity since well before the start of the millennium which has just ended, it is far older than Parliament, older even than the Kingdom of England itself. Even before the place we know as Essex emerged into history its varied landscape, coastline and numerous creeks and estuaries, had already attracted human settlement for millennia. *Splendid and Permanent Pageants* illustrates the County's past from the first farming communities more than 5000 years ago, through to the 20th century.

The County Council has played a major part in protecting and promoting the County's Heritage, employing staff with a wide range of specialist knowledge, of historic buildings, archaeology, and the historic landscape. These staff will have a key role to play in developing an interdisciplinary and sustainable approach to the historic environment in the 21st century.

Whilst the County Council has had, and will continue to play, a central role in caring for the County's past, it cannot successfully do so alone. Only through co-operation, with individuals, local societies and District Councils can the County's past be effectively understood, conserved and managed. Co-operation with the unitary authorities, London Boroughs and neighbouring Counties is also important, in order to ensure that areas of mutual concern, or issues which transcend administrative boundaries, are adequately dealt with.

The present book is a fine example of such co-operation. It is a pleasure to record the generous help of the many individuals, Local Authorities, and, of course, the artists in providing information and allowing pictures to be reproduced.

Finally this book is intended as a celebration of Essex history. Amidst all the current talk of conservation and sustainable management it is important to remember that the remarkable heritage which is all around us can be appreciated and enjoyed by all those who visit, travel through, and, most importantly, live in Essex. *Splendid and Permanent Pageants* will add to the enjoyment and appreciation of the County's past as we move into the 21st century.

ISBN 1 85281 209 5

"...pictures can be splendid and permanent pageants, not losing their power, but becoming more potent." - Alan Sorrell 1934

Contents

Historic sites

This map shows the extent of the historic County of Essex including Southend and Thurrock unitaries and those parts of the County which are now in Greater London.

The numbered boxes on the map of Essex indicate the approximate location of the illustrations by Figure number.

The past is all around us in many forms, old buildings, the patterns of fields and farms, earthworks and many kinds of archaeological remains and finds. Archaeological sites are often invisible from the ground and only discernible as fleeting marks in ripening crops visible on aerial photographs. Explaining what these places may have looked like in their heyday when they formed part of the living fabric of daily life, can be very difficult, particularly when dealing with the highly fragmentary remains revealed by archaeological excavation. One of the best and most vivid ways of doing this is to paint or draw a picture to show what the site might once have looked like. Such images can bring the past alive better than any written description, but it is worth remembering that these pictures are informed interpretations and only suggest what a place may have looked like at a particular time. Like any interpretation of historical events the pictures tell us as much about ourselves, and our own attitudes, as they do about the past.

A selection of some of the best archaeological and historical reconstruction pictures of Essex sites is presented in this book. It should be stressed that it is just a selection, for it is likely that there are more reconstruction pictures available for Essex than for any other English county. Indeed as the recently published book *City of Victory* (Crummy 1997) demonstrates, Colchester alone probably has more such pictures than many counties. Local authorities and related bodies, in particular Essex County Council, Southend Borough Council, Colchester Borough Council and the Colchester Archaeological Trust, have played a key role in commissioning these pictures. Some private individuals have also made significant contributions in supporting the Local Authorities before World War Two, and occasionally since the War in commissioning reconstructions to illustrate their own work.

Amongst the earliest reconstructions of Essex sites are pictures produced by Sir Charles Nicholson in the late 1920s of Barking Abbey and Prittlewell Priory, Southend (Figs 83 & 84). Nicholson had a thriving architectural practice, and was consulting architect for Lincoln, Wells, Lichfield, and Norwich Cathedrals and Diocesan architect for Wakefield and Chelmsford Cathedrals. As such he was keenly interested in, and had a great knowledge of, medieval architecture. He lived for many years at Porters, a large 16th-century house in Southend which was later sold to the Borough Council. Nicholson was very active in Essex, he designed the extension to the Cathedral at Chelmsford, and was closely involved in advising on the restoration of Prittlewell Priory (Johnston 1921-22, 54), which no doubt provided him with information and inspiration for his reconstruction picture. He was also a key figure in the foundation of the Southend-on-Sea and District Antiquarian and Historical Society (SDAHS), and became its first president. This society included many prominent local

1. Introduction

Fig 1. Southend Sorrell's preliminary oil sketch for the arrival of the first mail coach at Southend.

1

politicians and was an important link in the development of archaeological and historical reconstruction painting. The society was a key part of the milieu which led to Alan Sorrell's introduction to the world of reconstruction pictures. Sorrell dominated this field nationally throughout the middle decades of the 20th century and anyone who has ever visited a castle, ruined abbey or other archaeological site on public display almost anywhere in Britain is almost certain to have seen one of Sorrell's pictures.

The story of Sorrell's first attempts at reconstruction work have been described in some detail elsewhere (Sorrell, M. 1981). After studying at the Royal College of Art and the British School in Rome, he returned to England in 1931, with a plan to become involved in preparing mural paintings to adorn various public buildings. Sorrell approached the mayor of Southend with a plan to decorate the walls of the Central Library (now the Central Museum) in Victoria Avenue in the centre of Southend. Whilst agreement for this work was secured with "gratifying ease" (Sorrell, M. 1981, 9), it was not an entirely trouble-free process.

Sorrell, in line with a very modern 1930s view of the need for social relevance and realism in art, hoped to decorate the walls with scenes of contemporary life, but he was disappointed in this, and the pictures he produced were of historical scenes. In a little known essay written whilst Sorrell was actually engaged on the paintings, there are clear indications of how this drastic change of plan came about. Apparently when Sorrell "approached Alderman Martin (then Mayor of Southend) with a proposal to decorate the library, he referred me to Mr Pollitt, the Librarian who quickly became enthusiastic and introduced me to Mr J. W. Burrows J.P., a member of the Public Libraries and Museums Committee." (Sorrell 1934, 265-266). Both Pollitt and Burrows were leading figures in the SDHAS, both were Fellows of the Society of Antiquaries and had been closely involved with the restoration of Prittlewell Priory and other work on historic buildings in Southend. Furthermore both would probably have been familiar with the paintings being prepared to decorate the newly built Braintree Town Hall (Figs 3 - 9, Courtauld 1931). It is therefore unsurprising that these two dropped Sorrell's notion of contemporary pictures in favour of historical subjects. Four scenes were proposed, the pictures were to fit four elongated vertical spaces in the upper gallery of the Library, and were to show:-

The foundation of Prittlewell Priory (Fig. 2)

The building of Prittlewell Church tower (Fig. 92)

The refitting of Admiral Blake's fleet at Leigh (Fig. 99)

The arrival of the first Mail Coach at Southend (Fig. 112)

It is clear that at this stage Sorrell still cherished hopes of being able to paint

scenes of contemporary life. His essay ends hopefully with the thought that, "There are large round-topped spaces at each end of the gallery, and the scheme of decoration will not be complete until they too are filled with paintings, recording, perhaps, something of our own day. I cannot help thinking that the fantastic erection we call the 'Pier' should take its place in one of these spaces. The future will certainly regard this town on stilts as something quaint and old fashioned or as an extraordinary engineering feat. I do not know which it will be, but in either case Southenders of AD 2000 will be as grateful for a picture of the Pier as we should be for a large contemporary painting, of, say, Hadleigh Castle in King Richard's time" - this suggestion was not pursued (but see Fig.117).

Fig. 2

Sorrell's proposal for decorating the Library came just as the great economic depression of the 1930's began to hit home. Consequently, although the Library Committee wholeheartedly approved the proposal, the Borough Council did not feel it appropriate, given the grave financial situation, for expenditure to be devoted to this purpose (Sorrell 1934). Private sponsors were therefore sought; Burrows himself commissioned four relatively small oil sketches of the paintings to demonstrate the themes and general appearance of the finished paintings. One of these is reproduced here (Fig. 1) and it is interesting to compare with the finished painting (Fig 112).

Fig. 2. Prittlewell Sorrell's painting of the foundation of Prittlewell Priory in the early 11th century. The Prittle Brook is shown in the foreground and the first monks are arriving to take possession of the land. The ruins they are being ushered into are those of a Roman building. Construction work in the 1920's had revealed quantities of Roman brick and tile and this was taken to indicate the presence of a substantial Roman structure on the site (Pollitt 1935, 31-32).

All four pictures were eventually completed and displayed in the library as planned. They can now be seen in the Prittlewell Priory Museum in Southend. These pictures were Sorrell's first attempts at reconstruction painting, the first steps on a journey which eventually led to his virtual dominance of archaeological reconstruction painting after the Second World War (Sorrell, M. 1981, 9-19).

Anyone familiar with Sorrell's work will know the very distinctive windblown, brooding appearance of the scenes he painted, and the origins of this style can be traced to his view of the Essex landscape. This is indicated in his 1934 essay where he states that his pictures "express well the character of south-east Essex, watchfullness, angular active forms, scudding clouds and an easterly breeze" (Sorrell 1934). Such comments capture the tone of his pictures and it is pleasing to think that the bitter winds of an east Essex winter blow through all his paintings no matter what their geographical location.

Fig. 3. The Roman period is the earliest depicted in the Braintree Town Hall paintings. The town was known to be situated at a crossroads of Roman roads and Roman remains had been found in the Braintree area, but not in sufficient quantity for their character to be understood. Accordingly "This picture merely indicates that the Roman occupation of Britain definitely concerned Braintree. The artist has depicted a mounted Roman officer, a centurion and some British inhabitants" (Courtauld 1931). Archaeological work since the war has revealed much about Roman Braintree and a thriving small market town is now known to have existed around the Roman cross roads (Havis 1993; Medlycott 1999). To the right of the Roman picture, spread across two bays the artist has painted a late Saxon ploughing scene based closely on a manuscript illustration, accurately copying the form of the plough which is being pulled by oxen.

Fig. 4. The battle of Maldon, which took place in 991 between Viking raiders and the East Saxons led by Byrhtnoth, is celebrated in one of the most famous of Anglo-Saxon poems. As Courtauld (1931) pointed out, the connection between Braintree and the battle is that "a contingent from Braintree and its neighbourhood under Aethric, the local chieftain, fought at it". Aethric owned the manor of Bocking. The vigour of the painted figures and heap of bodies depicts something of the violence of the battle. However, although Courtauld (1931) says that, "The artist has taken great trouble to make the costumes, etc. in each picture correct for the period"; the charging Norsemen on the left of the picture with their elaborately winged or horned helmets, seem to owe more to the popular late 19th/early 20th century view of the Vikings than to any 10th century reality. Indeed to the modern viewer images of "Asterix" cartoons are almost inevitably called to mind (compare the more recent painting below, Fig. 69). Two of the Saxon defenders are shown holding aloft scimitar-like swords, which look as though they might have been lifted from Essex County Council's coat of arms. These arms depict three Seaxes a kind of short single edged sword used by the Saxons. However, far from illustrating Saxon weapons the County's arms reflect an early-17th century notion of what a seax looked like (Essex

Record Office 1997). The coat of arms of the East Saxon kingdom was invented by the 16th-century geographer and antiquary John Speed, in his 'History of Great Britaine' (Gurney-Benham 1933). The curious scimitar like form of the blades is typical of the weapons which adorned many 16th and 17th century pictures of the ancient inhabitants of Britain (Piggott 1989, 74-82). The seaxes being held aloft in the Braintree picture lack the prominent notches on the blades shown on the County Council's arms. However, although Essex County Council from its inception in 1889 used the arms, notches were not standard on the blades until much later (Essex Record Office 1997), perhaps after the formal grant of arms from the College of Arms to the County Council in 1932 (Gurney-Benham 1933). Actual Saxon seaxes can be seen on display at the Museum of London, ironically they were an earlier Saxon weapon and probably would not have been used by the late Saxon warriors at the Battle of Maldon.

Fig.5 On the north wall of the Town Hall, King John is shown presenting a charter to the Bishop of London granting the bishop the right to hold a weekly market and annual fair on his lands at Braintree.

Fig.6. Essex was at the forefront of the Protestant Reformation, and when the Roman Catholic religion was briefly restored during the reign of Queen Mary, a number of Protestant martyrs were executed at various locations around the county. The painting on the south wall depicts one such event, which took place on March 28th 1555 at Braintree about where the Town Hall now stands. The artist depicts bundles of firewood being placed around the unfortunate victim whilst two fanatical monks attempt to persuade him to recant at the last moment. A third monk standing behind the Sheriff's officer, who has just read the warrant of execution, looks far less certain about the dreadful event.

The decoration of public or semi-public buildings with mural paintings depicting past events was quite common in the 19th and early 20th century, for instance in the decoration of the Royal Exchange in London. In Essex, both the Braintree Town Council Chamber (Figs 3-9) and the Essex County Council Chamber (Figs 10-15) were decorated with a series of pictures showing historical scenes from the County's history. The decoration of both Council Chambers was paid for by W. J. Courtauld, whose family had been connected with Essex, and with Braintree in particular, for two hundred years, the family fortune having its origins in the local textile industry. The Courtaulds were great local philanthropists, and patrons of various artists and architects. W.J. Courtauld had served for many years on both Braintree Town Council and Essex County Council, and had paid for the design and construction of Braintree Town Hall during the 1920's; consequently it was natural for him to commission paintings to complete the decoration of the Council Chamber. The paintings were executed by Maurice Griffenhagen in 1929-30, formally presented to Braintree in 1930 and briefly described in a booklet by Courtauld (1931). Seven paintings depicting Braintree's past decorated round-topped alcoves between the walls and ceiling with a picture of the great botanist John Ray over the door (Fig. 9).

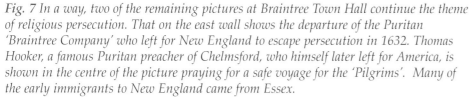

Fig. 7 In a way, two of the remaining pictures at Braintree Town Hall continue the theme of religious persecution. That on the east wall shows the departure of the Puritan 'Braintree Company' who left for New England to escape persecution in 1632. Thomas Hooker, a famous Puritan preacher of Chelmsford, who himself later left for America, is shown in the centre of the picture praying for a safe voyage for the 'Pilgrims'. Many of the early immigrants to New England came from Essex.

Fig. 8 By contrast, the west wall depicts Huguenots, Protestant refugees from France who fled to England to escape persecution by Louis XIV, many of whom took up residence in Essex, and are here shown weaving and dyeing. This picture reflects not only Braintree's long association with the textile industry, but the Courtauld's own family origins and their connection with silk production in the town.

Fig.9 John Ray was one of the greatest 17th-century scientists. Born at Black Notley, he became a fellow of Trinity College Cambridge in 1649, and returned to Essex in 1677, first to Faulkbourne Hall near Witham, and then to Black Notley. His botanical studies have led him to be widely regarded as the father of British botany.

When a new Council Chamber was being built for Essex County Council in the 1930's, the dire economic climate again caused problems. The story is told in a pamphlet published to celebrate the opening of the new Chamber in 1938; "When the Council Chamber plans were first put in hand it was necessary to keep a careful watch over the expense, and the Committee came to the conclusion that the task of making the Chamber and Lobby worthy of the County must be left to future generations. But the offer by councillor W. J. Courtauld was of such a character that the expert on County Halls Vincent Harris A.R.A. was, by arrangement, called in to advise in co-operation with the County Architect..." (Essex County Council 1939).

"A series of paintings were planned to show the history of the Essex people. The subjects for the pictures, portraits, historical scenes, and coats of arms, were suggested by a special Committee, but the individual artists who were commissioned were of course left free to paint them in their own way." (Essex County Council 1947).

Fig. 10. As with the Braintree pictures, the Roman period is the earliest depicted in the Essex County Council Chamber paintings. This is no surprise since in the 1930s the prehistory of Essex was, with some exceptions, virtually unknown. The great advances in our understanding of the county's prehistory is one of the triumphs of Essex archaeology over the last thirty years, and one in which the County Council has played a key role (Bedwin 1996; Hunter 1999, 43-46). The painting by C. Gill shows Boudica (Boudicea in 1938) at the sack of Colchester (see Fig. 45), and has a rather surreal, slightly nightmarish quality. Boudica, painted as a stern-faced thirties blonde, her foot resting on the severed head of one of her enemies, is surrounded by some of her warriors, and is about to pronounce the fate of a white haired Roman officer and a bound woman. In the background buildings burn and there are rather isolated images of dead bodies and violent struggle. It is interesting to compare this painting with the more recent and more naturalistic depiction of the sack of Colchester (Fig. 45).

Fig. 10

Fig. 11

Fig. 11. This picture by Fleetwood Walker shows John Ball preaching at Brentwood. John Ball, a priest of Colchester, was one of the leading figures in the Peasants' Revolt of 1381 against the Poll Tax. Essex people together with the people of Kent were at the forefront of the insurrection, and the first significant act of the revolt was an attack on the tax collectors sent to Brentwood to collect the new tax. John Ball is traditionally credited with having devised a slogan for the revolt "When Adam delved and Eve span, who was then the Gentleman?" Although there is no evidence that John Ball actually visited Brentwood, he preached widely in Essex, and the painter has brought together one of the leading figures of the revolt and its flashpoint.

Two large paintings decorated the stairs to the Council Chamber lobby (Figs 14 and 15). In the Chamber itself, the names of the Saxon kings of Essex were inscribed around the top of the walls and four large paintings (Figs 10-13) were placed on the long wall opposite the windows. The south wall is decorated with two maps one showing Essex in 1576, the other a contemporary map of the county in 1938. In between the maps were depicted the royal arms the arms of Essex and the arms of the county town, together with the crossed flags of the Essex Regiment. The spaces at either side of the two maps were decorated with the coats of arms of other Essex towns. The north wall was inscribed with the names of twenty-four famous Essex men and women, with the portraits of seven more Essex worthies above. One of these, William Morris, appropriately enough, was a great supporter of the "new County Councils" when they were first established in the late 1880s. He told the International Socialist Working Men's League in Paris in 1889 that the County Councils "seemed like being the germ of real local self-government" (MacCarthy 1994, 579-80). Morris would no doubt have approved the condition, "That only the best work and materials be accepted" that Courtauld attached to his gift.

Fig. 12

Fig. 12 As noted above, Essex was at the forefront of the Protestant Reformation in the 16th century and Puritan non-conformity in the 17th century. This picture by A. Thompson shows an Essex contingent of the Pilgrim Fathers being rowed towards the 'Mayflower'. The standing figure is Christopher Martin (the expedition's treasurer) from Billericay, his wife and two of his household are also shown. Given the pinched smile on the face of Martin's wife, it may be that the irony of having three female figures in the foreground of a painting of the 'Pilgrim Fathers' was not lost on the artist.

All these 1930s pictures reflect the tremendous pride taken by local politicians in the long and eventful history of the County. In effect they are paintings of historical scenes, and can be seen as late examples of the long tradition of history painting which had thrived during the previous two hundred years. Reconstruction pictures of more strictly archaeological subjects became more commonplace after the Second World War, when there was an upsurge in rescue excavations in the 50s, 60s and 70s. As noted above, Sorrell dominated this field, and fittingly the first post-war archaeological reconstruction paintings of Essex sites were the pictures he produced of Rayleigh Castle (Fig. 71, Sorrell, M. 1981). These pictures were informed by the excavations carried out under the auspices of the National Trust local committee between 1959-61 and 1969-70 (Helliwell and Macleod, 1981), and once again were private commissions. However, the majority of archaeological reconstruction paintings of Essex sites have been carried out by two artists, Frank Gardiner and Peter Froste. Many examples of their work can be seen in this book, and have been commissioned by Essex County Council beginning with a painting by Frank Gardiner of a prehistoric ceremonial monument, known as a cursus (Fig. 16), and excavated at Springfield in the early 1980s. Peter Froste's Essex pictures have been mostly commissioned by Colchester Borough Council and the Colchester Archaeological Trust, starting with a picture of the famous Balkerne Gate, the east gate of the Roman town of Colchester. Iain Bell, Roger Massey-Ryan and Nick Nethercoat of Essex County Council's

Fig. 13

Fig. 13. The final picture in the Council Chamber by R. Lyon shows Samuel Pepys, the famous diarist. He was Clerk of the King's Ships, and MP for Harwich, and is shown inspecting ships being built at Harwich. With him are Sir Anthony Deane the shipwright and the Duke of York, later James II. Pepys and Deane were friends, and Deane was also MP for Harwich. The construction of a ship illustrated by a wooden model is being discussed. Pepys found such models very useful and records in his diary, "Cooper came to me and began his lecture upon the body of a ship - which my having of a model in the office is of great use to me, and very pleasant and useful it is." Harwich was a major naval dockyard at the time and the town is visible in the background looking rather Mediterranean. Indeed the whole painting with its bright light, and blue sky seems very Mediterranean, even the figure in the prow of a boat on the right of the picture is reminiscent of a gondolier.

Heritage Conservation Branch have also produced many pictures. The tradition of more strictly historical reconstructions has been continued by Ashley Cooper, a farmer and local historian, who has commissioned the wildlife artist, Benjamin Perkins, to prepare many sketches and paintings (e.g. Figs 96, 113, 114) to illustrate books on the Gestingthorpe and Bulmer areas (e.g. Cooper 1994; 1998). All the paintings are the result of careful consideration of a wide range of evidence and represent the best view of what a site may have looked like at a particular point in time. In addition to these formal large scale paintings, many informal rapid sketches are produced to illustrate particular sites or finds, and these frequently appear in Essex County Council's annual newspaper supplement *Essex Past and Present* (formerly *Essex Archaeology*). Reconstruction paintings play a vital role in all kinds of books, leaflets and exhibitions in bringing to life the rich and varied history of Essex. The majority are traditional line drawings, watercolour or oil paintings, however computer generated images are beginning to be used (e.g. Figs 38, 80-82, 99 and 105). This field is sure to be developed as all those who care for the county's heritage continue to seek to preserve, understand and present its long and important history in the 21st century.

The two pictures in the Lobby of County Hall depict visits by two famous Queens. **Fig. 14** (below), by A. Lawrence, shows Elizabeth I visiting the army commanded by the Earl of Leicester assembled at Tilbury to repel the threatened Spanish invasion from the Low Countries (then part of the Spanish Empire) in 1588. The background shows a symbolic representation of what was being defended, and not what was visible from Tilbury. On the left behind the pikes and ship's sails are the white cliffs of Dover whilst to the right London is represented by the buildings shown clustered around Old St.Pauls.

Fig. 14

Fig. 15 (below) shows Victoria at Epping Forest in 1882 formally dedicating 5559 acres of forest for public enjoyment. This event followed a long struggle to prevent the Forest's destruction (Hunter 1999, 25-30), and the girl in the foreground is Victoria Buxton, daughter of one of the leading figures in the fight to preserve the forest. With the Queen in her carriage is her daughter Beatrice, and her famous servant John Brown is one of the two figures at the rear of the carriage.

Fig. 15

Farming was first introduced into Britain during the Neolithic period, an innovation which provided the foundation for all the remarkable social and economic developments of succeeding millennia. Before this, the economy was entirely based on hunting and gathering. Human groups were highly mobile exploiting resources in different parts of the landscape as they became available on a seasonal basis. Movement would have been through a well-known landscape within defined territories. The presence of these highly mobile communities is indicated by widespread scatters of distinctive tools made of struck flint. These collections of flints are concentrated on the sands and gravels, with major sites at Great Baddow, on the wooded hills of south-east Essex, and at sites, now within the intertidal zone but then on dry land, at Walton-on-the Naze, Fenn Creek in the Crouch estuary and Maylandsea in the Blackwater estuary.

During the Neolithic period, the sea level was much lower than today and sites within the present intertidal zone are remarkably well preserved, with extensive areas of old landsurface Figs 18 and 19). Pollen analysis of soils and recovery of preserved plant remains from these sites indicate no sudden switch to a purely farming economy; wild resources appear to have been at least as important as cultivated ones. A major innovation was the construction of monumental earthworks, and these sites have been the subjects of major excavations and reconstruction paintings.

A remarkable example lay in the Chelmer Valley close to modern Chelmsford. This site was identified from aerial photographs and partly excavated prior to its destruction by housing development. It comprised a large rectangular ditched enclosure about 670m long by 40m wide, running roughly east west along the valley. This type of monument is known as a Cursus, a name given to the first such enclosure identified near Stonehenge by the 18th century antiquary William Stukely. He chose the Latin for racecourse as a name since he interpreted the distinctive form of these strange sites as having been used by the Ancient Britons for horse and chariot races. Excavations showed that within the eastern end of the Springfield Cursus was a circular setting of large postholes which originally held upright timber posts. In addition, in the interior at this end of the Cursus were numerous pits, and a variety of formal deposits of pottery and other artefacts were made in these features and in the Cursus ditches themselves.

Fig. 16. Springfield This painting of the Neolithic Cursus as it may have appeared in use, shows a focus of activity at the timber circle inside the east end of the monument. Groups of people are shown entering the enclosed area at particular locations and moving along the length of the monument towards the eastern end.

2. Neolithic
(c.4000-2000BC)

Fig 16

Fig. 17 Orsett Causewayed Enclosure *This painting shows the causewayed ditches with a continuous bank between the outer ditches, backed by a palisade of upright wooden posts, together with large posts and screens controlling access to the interior. Within the inner enclosure which is marked out by another circuit of causewayed ditch and earth bank, a communal ceremony is shown taking place. At the same time a smaller group are carrying out a more private ritual placing artefacts within one of the ditches.*

Fig. 17

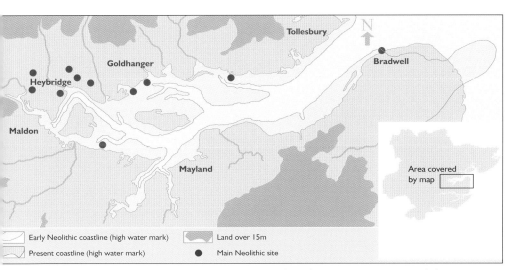

Early Neolithic coastline (high water mark)
Present coastline (high water mark)
Land over 15m
Main Neolithic site

Area covered by map

Tollesbury
Goldhanger
Bradwell
Heybridge
Maldon
Mayland

Fig. 18 Blackwater Estuary (left). Map showing the early Neolithic coastline of central Essex when the sea level was much lower. Sites now within the intertidal zone, but once on dryland, preserve a remarkable range of information which has been lost from sites which have remained on dry land.

Fig.19 The Stumble (below). Excavation of a Neolithic settlement site at the Stumble in the Blackwater estuary. The work had to be carried out in the intervals between tides.

Fig. 19

Fig. 20. Purfleet Neolithic polished flint and ground stone tools from a submerged forest in the Thames estuary at Purfleet.

At Orsett, on a gravel terrace overlooking the Thames, a major Neolithic monument has been recorded (Fig.17). Like so many archaeological sites in Essex this was identified as a cropmark from aerial photographs. The aerial view showed dark marks representing three concentric ditches with numerous interruptions or causeways. The two outer ditches were close together and backed by a narrow linear feature. The inner ditch lay some distance from the outer ditch circuits. Unlike the ditches, the accompanying banks seen to have been continuous. The interrupted ditches may have been the result of gang working, particular groups, perhaps related families, were assigned a particular length of ditch to dig to supply material for the bank. Such a method of working would certainly fit well with the notion of mobile family groups, coming together to create communal monuments. Such sites may represent one of the means through which individual groups were bound more closely into larger political units. Construction and use of monuments like Orsett and Springfield helped to bring larger communities into being and provided the stage on which communal bonds could be established, maintained and reworked.

Once dug, the ditches of causewayed enclosures became locations where carefully selected groups of objects including pottery, stone and flintwork were ceremonially deposited. Excavations at Orsett showed that the narrow linear feature visible on the aerial photograph inside the outer causewayed ditches was the foundation slot for a timber palisade. The excavations also showed that the main entrance was provided with large posts and wooden screens which would have channelled and controlled movement and access to the interior. A less complex causewayed enclosure has been excavated at Springfield Lyons overlooking the Cursus.

Fig. 20

15

Fig. 22. *Springfield* Reconstructed Neolithic pottery based on examples excavated from the Springfield Lyons causewayed enclosure. In the background is a stone saddle quern used for grinding grain, one of the pots is full of hazelnuts, and wild plants gathered for food lie to the left of the picture. Hazelnut shells are amongst the most common food remains recovered from Neolithic sites, although cereals were grown at this time. Evidence from sites like the Stumble (Fig. 19) indicate that wild plant foods remained at least as important as cultivated ones.

Fig. 22

1

Fig. 21 Brightlingsea (above) A Neolithic bowl excavated at Brightlingsea. This bowl is highly decorated and has a burnished surface; the vessel walls are very thin and the pot is skilfully made. The holes in the pot wall may have been made to allow a crack to be repaired with a leather or fabric binding. Above the pot, a top view of part of the rim is shown. The blank area represents a zone where part of the surface has been worn away. This damage may have resulted from the use of a lid or perhaps from this round-based pot being frequently stored upside down. This drawing is a good example of the 'technical' illustrations included in the formal reports on archaeological excavations.

Both the Springfield and Orsett sites continued to provide focal points in the landscape and locations for a range of activities into the Bronze Age. The Cursus became a focus for the construction of round barrows. Round barrows are amongst the most characteristic features of the Bronze Age. Similar monuments had been built during the Neolithic, and Early Neolithic examples have been excavated at Brightlingsea and Rainham. Round barrows comprised ditches surrounding mounds of earth, constructed over one or more burials either inhumations or cremations. Barrows could be complex monuments with mounds altered and enlarged, settings of timber posts, recut ditches and further burials added over many years.

3. Bronze Age
(c. 2000 - 750 BC)

Fig. 23 Dedham (right) Reconstruction of a round barrow excavated at Jupes Hill, Dedham. The picture shows the barrow's appearance after several generations of use, with the mound grassed over. A group of people is shown engaged in a ceremony involving the opening of part of the ditch and burial of a small pot as an offering.

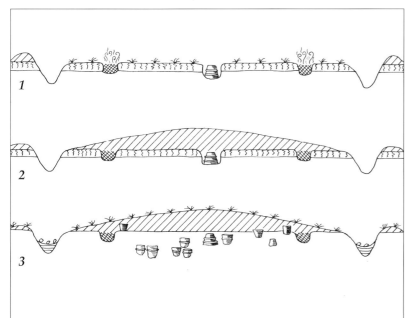

Fig. 24 Ardleigh (left) Sketch cross sections by Erith c. 1960, showing his interpretation of how one of the Ardleigh burial mounds developed in the Bronze Age.
(1) The first stage was a circular ditched enclosure; a central cremation burial was placed beneath an urn and two pits dug and fires lit within them.
(2) Subsequently a mound was heaped over the central burial and the pits, creating a barrow.
(3) Over a number of generations, many other cremation burials accompanied by urns were buried within the mound, other deposits being made in the partly silted ditches.

Often, after centuries of ploughing all that remains of round barrows are circular ditches, known as ring-ditches, which are often visible as cropmarks. In north-east Essex very dense clusters of ring ditches are known mainly from aerial photographs, a number have been excavated including one at Brightlingsea close to the Early Neolithic monument. However the classic example is at Ardleigh. This site was first investigated by local farmer Felix Erith, who together with the Colchester Archaeological Group in the later 1950s and early 1960s excavated many of the ring-ditches. Since then further work at the site, both aerial photography and further excavation, has revealed the remarkable complexity of this cemetery (Brown 2000).

Fig. 25 Ardleigh Part of the large cemetery at Ardleigh as it might have looked during use. In this cemetery and others like it, cremation burials were placed around or within ring-ditches of various sizes, which might or might not be provided with mounds. Ring-ditches and mounds may have formed circumscribed areas or platforms, within or on which particular actions could be carried out. Over time, an elaborate and distinctive cemetery maze-like topography was created which determined access routes to the place of burial. As this picture shows the sheer density of ring-ditches and mounds may have at least partially obscured any view from the east. The arrangement of the major Bronze Age boundaries known at Ardleigh, together with the indications of settlement locations, make it likely that the main approach to the cemetery would have been from the east. It would have been virtually impossible to walk through the cemetery in a straight line. Anyone approaching from or returning to the east would be diverted along often very narrow paths around the numerous ring-ditches. This circuitous route of approach and departure may have been of considerable symbolic importance.

Fig. 25

Fig. 26 Ardleigh This picture gives an idea of the landscape at Ardleigh in about 1200BC. The cemetery is shown in the centre foreground. This together with two major linear ditches, known from cropmarks and partly excavated in 1980, defined a large area of flat land between a tributary of the Salary Brook and the headwaters of the Bromley Brook. There are only slight hints of the likely locations of houses and the core of the settlement at Ardleigh. Accordingly the buildings fields and paddocks shown in the foreground are largely based on evidence from elsewhere. Between this settlement core and the major linear ditch to the north, an area of controlled grazing and stock management is shown, with open grazing and woodland beyond.

The later Bronze Age is the first period in which evidence of houses, farms, fields and the agricultural economy is relatively plentiful.

Many Late Bronze Age (1000-750BC) settlements have been excavated in Essex, particularly in the south and east of the county. A good example is at Lofts Farm situated on the gravel terraces north of the Blackwater estuary. Here a double ditched enclosure was excavated in advance of gravel extraction. Within the enclosure a range of postholes were recorded, the remains of the timber uprights of a variety of buildings including a central roundhouse. Most of the buildings were in the southern part of the enclosure, which was cut in two by a fence line running from the entrance east-west behind the central roundhouse. The building included a number of two- and four-post structures, and in the south-east corner a long rectangular building. There was a distinctive distribution of finds from around this building. Fragments of pottery and other domestic debris were frequent from the western end but absent from the east; a gully

running from this eastern end into one of the enclosure ditches may have been a drain. This evidence indicates the building was used as a longhouse with people living at the west end and livestock at the eastern end. Plant remains, together with similar evidence from nearby sites, indicate that grain was brought to the site already processed. They also show that the local landscape consisted of open damp grassland with some scrub, perhaps hedges, and areas of oak woodland.

Fig. 27 Heybridge (left) Plan of the Lofts Farm settlement showing the Bronze Age enclosure ditches, pits and postholes are shown in green. The postholes around 1 are the remains of a central roundhouse which can be seen in the centre of the reconstruction painting (Fig. 29), and the group of postholes at 2 indicate the position of the longhouse shown in the foreground of the painting. Numbers 4-10 are four and two-post structures used for storage and drying. Number 11 indicates the postholes of a fenceline which divided the site in two, the fence probably ran right across the site but limited time for the excavations did not allow its east and west ends to be recorded. Number 12 indicates the postholes of the gate structure partly destroyed by a gravel company test pit prior to excavation.

Fig.28 Rochford (below) Although apparently a scene from the Australian outback this photograph is actually Wallasea island in about 1940. What is shown in this picture, a rather rough wooden fence, a large herd of livestock shepherded by two men on horseback aided by a dog, would probably not have surprised a Late Bronze Age inhabitant of Essex. This kind of scene would have been a familiar one on the Essex marshes from at least the Bronze Age down to the middle of the 20th century.

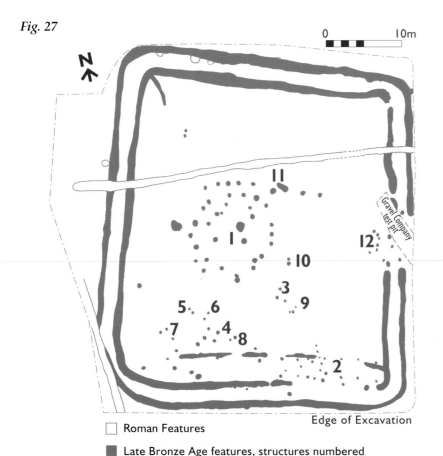

Fig. 27

0   10m

N

Gravel Company
test pit

Edge of Excavation

☐ Roman Features

■ Late Bronze Age features, structures numbered

Fig. 28

20

Fig. 29 Heybridge *This picture of the Lofts Farm enclosure as it may have been in about 850BC, shows the central roundhouse, the east-west fence line and the longhouse in the south-east corner. The two and four-post structures have been interpreted as storage facilities and drying racks. The site is low-lying with a high water-table particularly in winter, and storage in pits dug into the subsoil, which appears to have been a common practice during the Bronze and Iron Ages, would not have been practical. Similarly, the double enclosure ditches may have been a way of keeping the enclosure relatively dry. The damp grassland would have provided valuable grazing for livestock, as would the saltmarsh fringing the Blackwater to the south. The Essex salt marshes were widely used for grazing in later periods. A number of prehistoric wooden structures have been recorded during survey work in the Crouch and Blackwater, and have been interpreted by analogy with medieval and later practice as bridges to link areas of saltmarsh across narrow creeks.*

Amongst the most striking of Late Bronze Age settlements is a class of circular enclosure which occur throughout eastern England from Kent and Surrey up to Yorkshire. There are probably more such sites known in Essex than in any other county. Six of the Essex sites have been excavated, and a number of others are known from aerial photographs. They are generally located on elevated positions commanding extensive views.

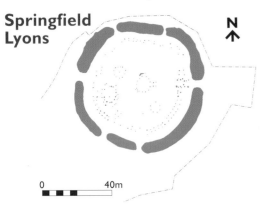

Springfield Lyons

N

0   40m

Fig. 30 Springfield Plan of the fully excavated enclosure at Springfield Lyons near Chelmsford. At this site, the Bronze Age circular ditch was originally dug in segments with numerous causeways. The double row of postholes running around the inside of the enclosure ditch represents the remains of a timber revetment for an earth bank. The group of large postholes at the main east facing entrance indicate the former presence of a large gate structure. Within the enclosure the roughly circular arrangements of postholes are the locations of roundhouses, the central one with an elongated porch structure facing the main east entrance to the enclosure.

Fig. 31 Springfield This painting depicts Springfield Lyons as it may have appeared about 850BC. It shows the site's prominent location overlooking the Chelmer valley, and the imposing nature of the bank, timber rampart and gatehouse at the east entrance. All these features present a marked contrast with the contemporary site at Lofts Farm (Fig. 29).

Fig. 32

*Fig.32 **Springfield** (above) Photograph of part of the enclosure ditch at Springfield Lyons being recorded during the course of excavation.*

*Fig. 33 **Springfield** (right). During the Late Bronze Age there is a marked change in pottery used compared to the Middle Bronze Age. The excavated sites produce large quantities of ceramic refuse, including not only large storage and cooking pots but many very fine jars, bowls and cups, suggesting a much greater emphasis during the Late Bronze Age on the presentation of food and drink. These reconstructed pots are based on excavated examples from Springfield Lyons.*

Fig. 33

All the Late Bronze Age circular enclosures share much in common, notably their circular form the choice of location and the range and type of artefacts present. However, despite these similarities, there are clear differences in internal arrangements.

Fig. 34 Mucking This reconstruction drawing shows an enclosure at Mucking overlooking the Thames estuary. This site, known as the North Ring, is one of two circular enclosures excavated at Mucking. Whilst the similarity with Springfield Lyons is clear, there are a number of differences; for instance at Mucking the bank lacks a timber revetment. The most striking difference lies in the approach to the internal buildings: at Springfield Lyons, anyone coming through the main east facing entrance would have been immediately faced with the elongated porch of the central roundhouse. By contrast, at Mucking North Ring the visitor would be confronted by a large wooden screen or fence with the buildings behind it.

4. Iron Age (750 BC - 43AD)

Fig 35

During the Iron Age settlement on the Boulder Clays of central and north-west Essex appears to have intensified. A major campaign of archaeological fieldwork in advance of the development of Stansted Airport as the third London airport during the 1980s revealed a range of interesting Iron Age sites. At the Carpark I Site (CIS) a rectilinear enclosure of Middle Iron Age date was excavated. This site was surrounded by a bedding trench for a palisade or fence. The trench became much deeper at the corners and at the entrance. At one point a pottery jar had been placed at the bottom of the trench perhaps as a foundation offering.

Fig. 35 Stansted (above) The reconstruction drawing shows the boundary of the CIS enclosure marked by a fence, with the corners and entrances marked by a much more substantial timber palisade. The animal skull shown on top of one of the posts at the entrance is a reminder of the symbolic importance of boundaries. Selected animal, and indeed human, bones were often placed in significant locations within and around prehistoric settlements. Inside the enclosure four-post rectangular storage buildings, like those at the Bronze Age site at Lofts Farm (Fig. 29), are shown, with a large circular roundhouse in the north-west corner opposite the entrance. A range of domestic activities are taking place in the eastern part of the enclosure, with the western part used as a farmyard.

Another of the sites recorded at Stansted, known as the Airport Catering Site (ACS), is one of the most completely excavated Late Iron Age settlements in Essex. The site was defined by a large rectilinear ditch, with a series of circular gullies around the inside, marking the sites of roundhouses. Towards the centre of the enclosure was a rectangular building, perhaps a shrine, with a linear feature running north-south linking it to the entrance, and dividing the enclosure in two. Amongst the finds recovered from the site were large quantities of pottery including fragments of wine storage jars imported from the Roman Empire. Coinage was first used in Britain during the later Iron Age and a hoard of potin (a type of bronze) coins was recovered from one of the house gullies. The plant remains and animal bone recovered from the site indicate a predominantly pastoral economy.

25

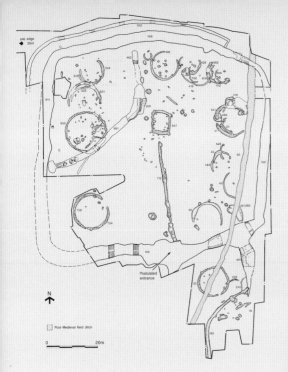

Fig. 36 Stansted (above) The plan of the excavated features shows that the settlement at the Airport Catering Site did not remain static. For instance many of the circular house gullies overlap showing that houses were rebuilt on slightly different alignments, and at some point the enclosure was subdivided with an internal ditch creating a roughly rectangular enclosure inside the north-west corner.

Fig. 37 Stansted (right) This reconstruction painting shows the enclosure protected by its substantial ditch with an internal bank topped by a wooden palisade, the roundhouses around the edge of the enclosure and the rectangular building, perhaps a shrine, in the centre.

Fig. 38 Stansted (right) Comparison of this with the previous picture is instructive. The painting was prepared during the course of the excavation to publicise the discovery of the settlement, whilst the second was prepared when the publication report was nearing completion. It was originally thought that the trench around the central rectangular building was a drainage gully as shown in the first picture. Further study indicated that this feature was more likely to represent a foundation trench for the walls as shown in the second picture, which also shows a major fence line linking the gate to the central rectangular building, and dividing the enclosure in two. The first picture like almost all the others in this book is a traditional painting the second is a computer-generated image.

Fig. 37

Fig. 39

The first stages of the development of towns took place in Britain during the Late Iron Age and one of the earliest and most important of these proto-urban sites was at Colchester, enabling the present town to proudly announce itself as "Britain's oldest recorded town". However, Iron Age Colchester, then known as Camulodunum, was not a densely built up place concentrated in one area. Occupation spread between the Colne and Roman rivers with two major centres, one at Sheepen and another at Gosbecks about 4km to the south. The Sheepen settlement was a kind of industrial centre with Gosbecks a primarily residential, agricultural and probably also a market, centre. Numerous items imported from the Roman Empire have been recovered from these sites.

Colchester was protected by an extensive series of large ditches and earth banks, known as dykes, running between the Colne and Roman rivers. These seem to have been intended to prevent any direct attack by forces using chariots or mounted on horseback. The entrances and gaps between the dykes enabled mobile defending forces to charge out and catch attackers unawares.

Fig. 39 Ilford (above). Uphall Camp lies on a gravel spur above marshy ground to the east of the River Roding in Ilford. The site was surrounded by a bank and ditch, with an additional bank on the western side. An area of about 24 ha was enclosed making Uphall the largest site of its kind in Essex. Much of the enclosure is now built over, but excavations have revealed the presence of roundhouses, rectangular buildings and stock enclosures. It is unlikely that the enclosure was totally filled with buildings, and as this painting shows there would have been small fields, stock pens and other open spaces as well as many buildings inside the earthwork defences.

Fig. 40 Harlow Temple (right) Excavations at this site have shown that in the Iron Age, a pair of roundhouses were built on the neck of a spur of high ground. These buildings were a focus of ritual deposition of objects including many coins. The roundhouses were built adjacent to a Bronze Age cemetery which had occupied a bowl barrow, the saucer like depression in the ground shown to the right of the two roundhouses. Veneration of Bronze Age sites and objects during the Iron Age seems to have been a common phenomenon. A late Bronze Age axe was included amongst the grave goods in the Lexden burial (Fig. 42).

Fig. 40

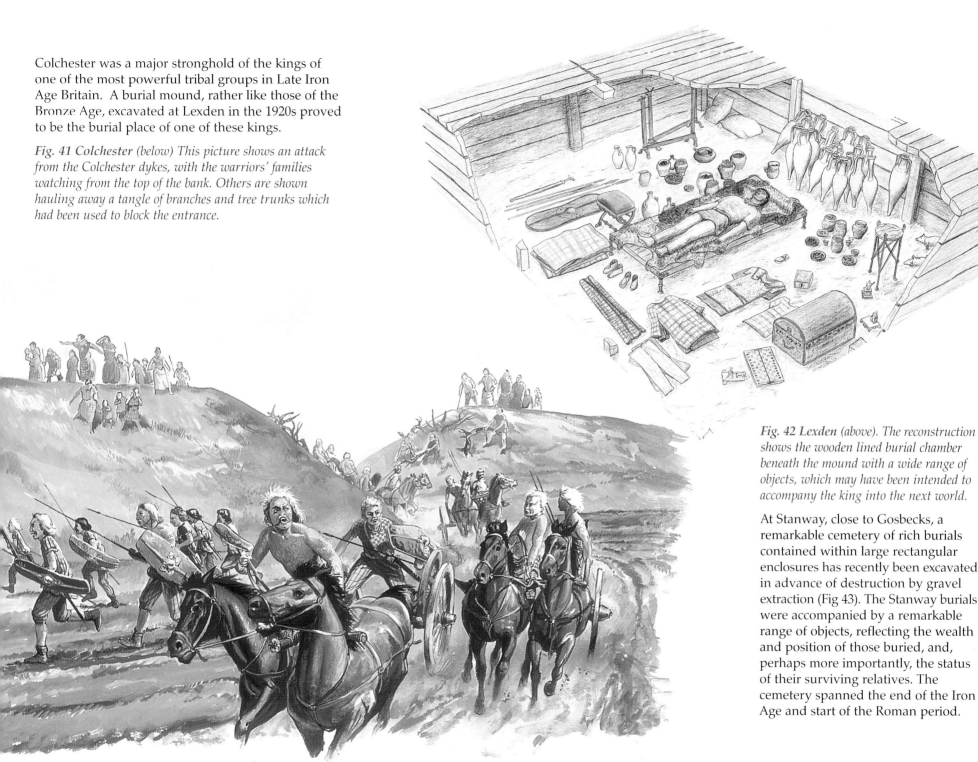

Colchester was a major stronghold of the kings of one of the most powerful tribal groups in Late Iron Age Britain. A burial mound, rather like those of the Bronze Age, excavated at Lexden in the 1920s proved to be the burial place of one of these kings.

Fig. 41 Colchester (below) This picture shows an attack from the Colchester dykes, with the warriors' families watching from the top of the bank. Others are shown hauling away a tangle of branches and tree trunks which had been used to block the entrance.

Fig. 42 Lexden (above). The reconstruction shows the wooden lined burial chamber beneath the mound with a wide range of objects, which may have been intended to accompany the king into the next world.

At Stanway, close to Gosbecks, a remarkable cemetery of rich burials contained within large rectangular enclosures has recently been excavated in advance of destruction by gravel extraction (Fig 43). The Stanway burials were accompanied by a remarkable range of objects, reflecting the wealth and position of those buried, and, perhaps more importantly, the status of their surviving relatives. The cemetery spanned the end of the Iron Age and start of the Roman period.

29

Fig. 43 This reconstruction shows a cremation taking place at Stanway, note the round and rectangular burial mounds inside two of the large enclosures.

30

5. The Roman Period (AD43 - 410)

Fig. 44

Fig. 44 Colchester (above). This picture shows the legionary fortress in AD48; this fortress with its grid pattern of roads, barracks and administrative buildings was quite unlike anything previously seen in Britain. It was carefully sited on a prominent spur overlooking the River Colne. The purpose of the smaller rectangular annex shown on the right-hand side of the picture is uncertain.

When the Roman army invaded Britain in AD43, Colchester was a prime target. After the initial invasion and crossing of the Thames, the army was joined by the emperor Claudius himself, and, complete with a number of war elephants, advanced through Essex to attack Colchester. Colchester was captured and the bulk of the invasion force moved on. However, a large force, probably the XX Legion, remained at Colchester and built a legionary fortress which occupied what is now the western half of the town centre.

As the conquest of Britain progressed and fighting moved to the north and west the XX Legion was moved to a new base and its fortress at Colchester was converted into a Roman town.

The continuation of wealthy burials at Stanway after the Roman Conquest indicates that there was some accommodation between the old and new rulers. However, increasing harshness in land appropriation, taxation and particularly in dealing with the semi-autonomous tribe of the Iceni, which occupied what is now Norfolk and part of Suffolk, led to unrest. This resulted in a violent revolt led by Boudica queen of the Iceni in AD 60. Colchester provided a focus for native anger, without town walls and with a very small garrison it was attacked, burned to the ground and its inhabitants slaughtered.

Fig. 45 Colchester The Roman historian Tacitus describes the inhabitants of Colchester retreating to the great stone built Temple of Claudius as a place of last refuge. This graphic painting shows the British warriors gathering for a final assault on the Temple at the edge of the burning town. Compare this scene with the painting from the Essex County Council Chamber (Fig 10).

The Britons went on to attack and destroy the Roman towns at London and St Albans, before being defeated in a pitched battle with the Roman army possibly near Mancetter in Warwickshire. Following the rebellion, peace was eventually restored to southern Britain and Colchester was rebuilt. This time, it was surrounded by a wall.

Fig. 46

Fig. 46 Colchester The western side of the town during the rebuilding; a substantial V shaped ditch was dug in front of the wall which is shown under construction. Colchester was the first Roman town in Britain to be provided with a wall, which was originally about 2.4m thick, 6m high and 2,800m long. The main western gate shown here and now known as the Balkerne Gate incorporated a major triumphal arch, which had probably been built to commemorate Claudius' victory.

Fig. 47 Colchester (below). The Balkerne Gate in use. This picture shows a flock of sheep and other agricultural produce being brought into the town. Throughout its history one of the major functions of the Roman town of Colchester would have been as a market centre. This picture is the first reconstruction painted by Peter Froste.

33

Fig. 48

Fig. 48 Colchester (above). Detailed view of the Balkerne Gate, showing the triumphal archway incorporated in the centre of the gate. The arch was faced with neatly dressed tufa stone probably quarried in Hampshire and shipped round the coast to Colchester. The stone of the arch contrasts with the horizontal tile bands of the new wall. The remains of the Balkerne gate can still be seen close to the Mercury Theatre and the Hole-in-the-Wall pub on Balkerne Hill.

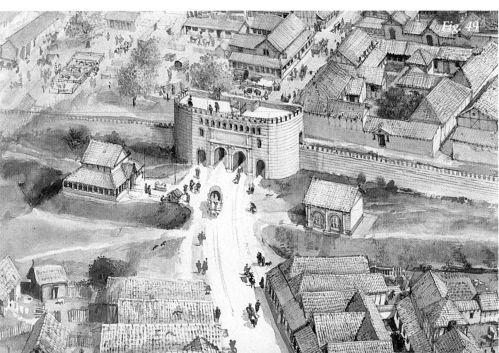

Fig. 49

Fig. 49 Colchester (below) The western side of the town as it may have appeared at the end of the first century AD showing the Balkerne gate and suburban development along the road leading to the town. In the centre background close to the gate, the building with a colonnaded verandah is a temple, and the building on the other side of the road may also have been a temple or shrine. The open area within the walls to the left of the gate is shown with pens for animals perhaps awaiting sale or slaughter.

Fig. 50 Colchester (right) This picture shows Colchester as it may have been about AD 250 with ordered streets surrounded by a stone wall. The rebuilt temple of Claudius and a D-shaped theatre can be seen in the centre right of the picture.

The important Iron Age centre at Gosbecks retained its religious, market and administrative functions during the Roman period. However, its appearance changed dramatically (Fig. 51); a major temple was built with a portico, a covered walkway rather like the cloisters attached to medieval abbeys. A theatre much larger than the one built within the walls of Colchester was constructed at Gosbecks.

Fig. 50

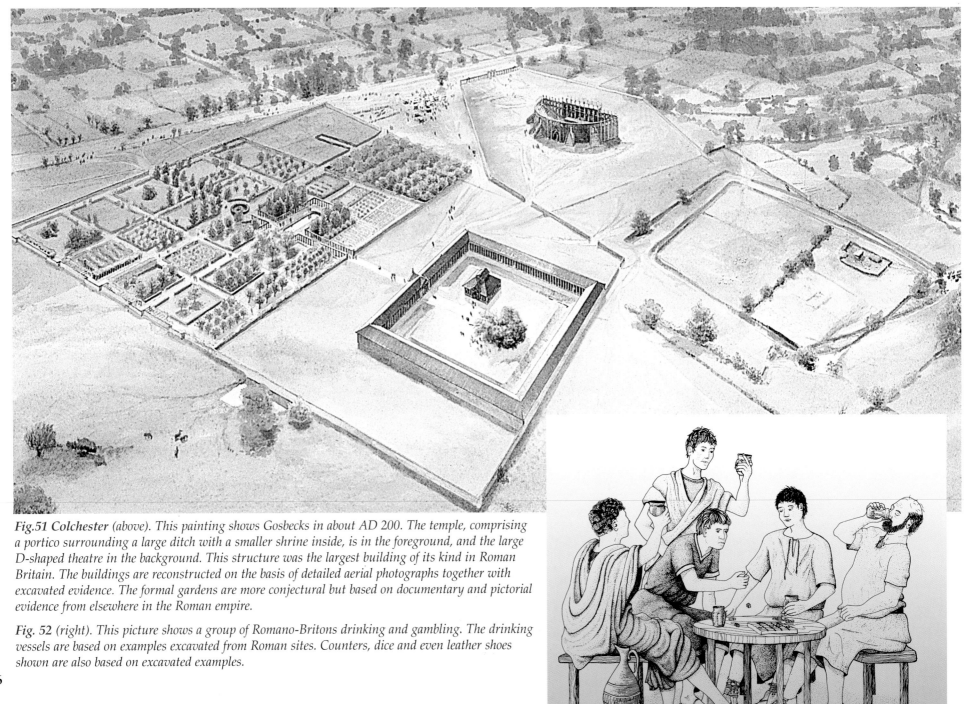

Fig.51 Colchester (*above*). *This painting shows Gosbecks in about AD 200. The temple, comprising a portico surrounding a large ditch with a smaller shrine inside, is in the foreground, and the large D-shaped theatre in the background. This structure was the largest building of its kind in Roman Britain. The buildings are reconstructed on the basis of detailed aerial photographs together with excavated evidence. The formal gardens are more conjectural but based on documentary and pictorial evidence from elsewhere in the Roman empire.*

Fig. 52 (*right*). *This picture shows a group of Romano-Britons drinking and gambling. The drinking vessels are based on examples excavated from Roman sites. Counters, dice and even leather shoes shown are also based on excavated examples.*

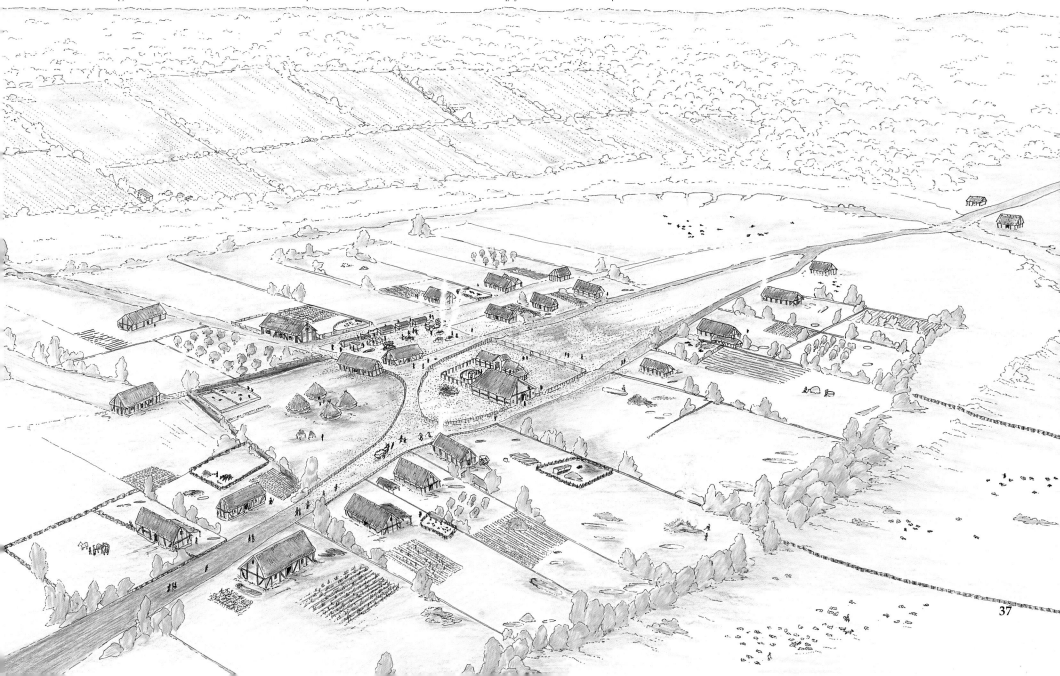

Fig 53 Heybridge Amongst the smaller 'towns' one of the most extensively excavated is at Elms Farm, Heybridge, where large-scale excavations took place prior to housing development. This shows the settlement, which appears to have developed around a temple or religious centre shown at the centre of the painting. Unlike Colchester this site was not provided with a wall and the roads were less rigidly gridlike. The settlement at Heybridge developed from Iron Age beginnings and probably served as a religious and market centre for the surrounding area, the Elms Farm site was well placed to exploit the Blackwater estuary for trade and transport.

37

The small town at Chelmsford known during the Roman period as Caeseromagus has been extensively excavated. It was strategically placed between the major Roman towns at London and Colchester and the main public building was the mansio, an official building for housing travelling government officials.

Fig. 54 Chelmsford (below) shows a reconstruction of the mansio based on excavated evidence. This building was a kind of posting station and administrative centre for government officials. It was provided with a bathhouse shown at the rear of the painting and stood within its own large precinct, hence the rather rural setting shown in this picture.

Fig. 55

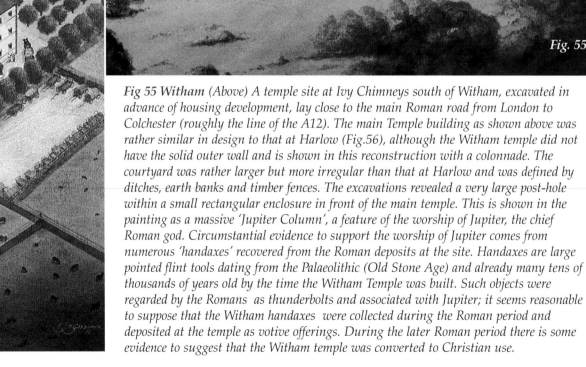

Fig 55 Witham (Above) A temple site at Ivy Chimneys south of Witham, excavated in advance of housing development, lay close to the main Roman road from London to Colchester (roughly the line of the A12). The main Temple building as shown above was rather similar in design to that at Harlow (Fig.56), although the Witham temple did not have the solid outer wall and is shown in this reconstruction with a colonnade. The courtyard was rather larger but more irregular than that at Harlow and was defined by ditches, earth banks and timber fences. The excavations revealed a very large post-hole within a small rectangular enclosure in front of the main temple. This is shown in the painting as a massive 'Jupiter Column', a feature of the worship of Jupiter, the chief Roman god. Circumstantial evidence to support the worship of Jupiter comes from numerous 'handaxes' recovered from the Roman deposits at the site. Handaxes are large pointed flint tools dating from the Palaeolithic (Old Stone Age) and already many tens of thousands of years old by the time the Witham Temple was built. Such objects were regarded by the Romans as thunderbolts and associated with Jupiter; it seems reasonable to suppose that the Witham handaxes were collected during the Roman period and deposited at the temple as votive offerings. During the later Roman period there is some evidence to suggest that the Witham temple was converted to Christian use.

Another small town which like Heybridge grew up around a temple site was Harlow. The Harlow Temple was a major structure which occupied the site of an Iron Age shrine (Fig 40) which has produced a great number of Iron Age coins, many in mint condition.

Fig. 56 Harlow Temple This painting based on excavations at the site shows the temple as it may have looked about AD 200. The site lay on a slight hill or spur and the temple building was set within a large walled courtyard. The buttresses on the courtyard wall in the foreground of the picture provided extra support where the wall approached the sloping edge of the hill.

Fig. 56

Fig. 57

Fig. 59 Chignall St James (right) This reconstruction shows the villa based on the cropmark and excavated evidence. The villa building itself was probably of some architectural pretension, no doubt reflecting the status of its owners. The large barn, trackway and paddocks shown in the foreground were recorded during the excavations.

Fig. 57 Colchester (above) Christian worship in the later Roman period is best represented in Essex by a remarkable building excavated at Butt Road, Colchester. This building aligned east-west was associated with a cemetery and almost certainly represents one of the earliest churches to be built in Britain. The remains of the building are displayed adjacent to the police station at Butt Road and this painting shows the church as it may have appeared in its heyday in the late 4th century, with plastered and whitewashed walls and red tiled roof.

Roman villas are probably the most famous type of Roman site, and some of the best evidence of Roman villas in Essex comes from sites to the north of Chelmsford.

Fig. 58 Chignall (right) This photograph shows a very clear cropmark of a villa building at Chignall St. James. The building plan around a central courtyard together with the internal wall divisions can all be seen. The villa cropmark is a Scheduled Ancient Monument but excavations south of the cropmark prior to gravel extraction revealed the fields, trackways and agricultural buildings which surrounded the main villa building.

Fig. 59

Fig. 60

Another extensively excavated villa, once again recorded in advance of gravel extraction, is that at Great Holts, Boreham. The villa here was very different in plan to that at Chignall St. James. The main building at Great Holts were all in line rather than ranged around a courtyard.

Fig. 60. Great Holts The excavations did not produce a great deal of roof tile, and it seems that only the bathhouse to the right of the main building was provided with a tiled roof, perhaps due to the greater risk of fire. This picture shows the main structure thatched, and the enclosures outside the building are shown as a busy farmyard, with water drained from the bathhouse channelled by a lined drain to a series of ponds in the foreground of the picture. However, the rather rustic appearance of the building should not obscure the status of the owners. Plant and bone remains indicate an extensive and varied diet including luxury items such as pine nuts, olives and grapes imported from the Mediterranean.

6. The Saxon Period (AD410 - 1066)

Fig. 61 Blackwater Estuary Reconstruction of one of a number of later Saxon fish-weirs in the Blackwater estuary (page 45). The large V shaped structure of substantial timber uprights linked by wattle panels channelled fish into a net attached to the end of the V. The trapped fish could then be collected at low-tide. This picture shows the fish being collected and the trap being repaired

With the decline of the Roman Empire in the 4th and 5th centuries AD, Britain became increasingly threatened by barbarian tribes from outside the Empire. The geographical position of Essex, together with its long coastline and numerous creeks and estuaries, made it particularly vulnerable to attack from across the North Sea. German tribes, the Saxons, Angles and Jutes from what are now South Denmark, North Germany and The Netherlands, were raiding eastern England at this time. One of the largest and earliest Saxon settlements known in England has been excavated at Mucking on a gravel terrace overlooking the Thames estuary.

The excavations at Mucking were amongst the largest ever carried out in Britain, and revealed a very extensive Early Saxon settlement with two large cemeteries. The settlement consisted of over 250 buildings, many of which were sunken-featured huts (Fig 63). These were buildings constructed over a rectangular pit dug into the subsoil; in some cases this pit was covered with a plank floor, but in most instances the bottom of the pit seems to have formed the floor of the building. There were also larger rectangular buildings constructed around a frame of substantial timber posts set into the ground. These 'halls' may have been

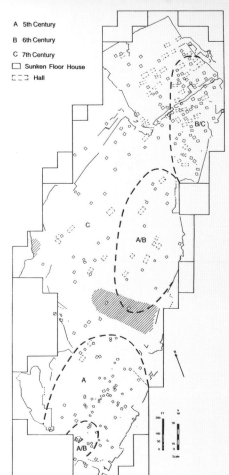

A 5th Century
B 6th Century
C 7th Century
☐ Sunken Floor House
⊏⊐ Hall

occupied by wealthier or higher status families within the settlement. The excavations have shown that not all the buildings were in use at the same time, and that the focus of the settlement shifted a number of times during the three hundred or so years that the site was occupied.

Fig. 62 (left) Simplified plan showing the shifting focus of the Mucking settlement from the early 4th to late 7th century AD.

Fig. 63 Mucking (right). This winter scene shows the north-eastern part of the settlement at Mucking. The reed marsh in the background occupies the lower ground, below the gravel terrace. The smaller buildings are the sunken-featured huts, some shown with short plank built walls, others with earth heaped up around the edges of the pits and the roof coming down to form a tent-like structure.

Fig. 64 Heybridge (below) Exterior of a sunken-featured building based on an example excavated at Elms Farm near Maldon.

Fig. 65 Colchester (above) View of a sunken-featured building as part of a farm based on evidence from Colchester.

Fig. 66 (right). Artists impression of the interior of one of the Saxon 'halls' at Mucking.

Investigations around the Blackwater estuary have revealed a remarkable range of evidence of Saxon occupation. Most striking and most famous is the 7th century church at Bradwell. Now starkly isolated on the edge of the marshes, its original position was far from lonely. The Blackwater was a major focus of activity during the later Saxon period. Settlements involved with extensive ironworking are known on the north bank. There was a royal centre at Brightlingsea and important estates are known to have existed on Mersea. In the estuary itself numerous large fish-traps or weirs are now known which have been radiocarbon dated to the later Saxon period (Fig. 61). Tree-ring dating has shown that the earliest timbers from the Strood causeway linking Mersea to the mainland are also of this date.

Long before any Saxon settlements had been excavated in Essex, a wide range of burials had been recognised. The most remarkable of the Saxon graves in the county was uncovered by workmen digging gravel at Broomfield in 1888. This was a princely burial accompanied by many gravegoods, comparable to those recovered from the famous Sutton Hoo ship burial. Unfortunately, because of the nature of the discovery and the conservation techniques available at the time, many of the organic artefacts present in the grave, including wooden bowls and a variety of textiles, are not preserved. The majority of the other finds are now in

Fig. 67 Alresford Reconstruction of a Saxon burial at Alresford, with the body wrapped in cloth lying in the grave, and grieving relatives placing wooden poles over the body.

the British Museum. Other cemeteries range from large examples such as those at Mucking to small groups of burials like one excavated at North Shoebury. The cemeteries generally comprise a mixture of cremation and inhumation burials.

The siting of many of these Saxon cemeteries is of some interest. They often seem to avoid Roman sites and are instead placed in much earlier monuments. This occurred at Ardleigh, and most dramatically at Orsett where Saxon burials were placed under barrows built within the causewayed enclosure, and at Springfield Lyons where the Bronze Age enclosure became the focus for an early Saxon cemetery. The major prehistoric earthworks at these sites would still have been clearly visible in the Early Saxon period. The location of the Saxon burials seems to represent a deliberate attempt by a new social order to forge a link with a remote past. One of the most unusual Saxon burials from Essex was excavated at Alresford. Here soil stains indicate that the body was placed in a blanket or winding sheet, with a wooden support for the head and the body covered with a series of close set wooden poles (Fig 67). This arrangement appears to be unique, although it is interesting to note that the record of the Broomfield burial states that the cloth items in the grave were laid on top of birchwood logs set close together and lying east-west.

Fig. 68 Wicken Bonhunt
A large later Saxon site was excavated at Wicken Bonhunt, prior to construction of the M11. This painting shows the orderly arrangement of rectangular structures revealed by the excavations. The site was partly surrounded by a small stream, and partly demarcated by a timber palisade, the painting shows a watermill on the stream in the foreground. In the background within the enclosure can be seen a large cemetery which contained many hundreds of graves.

47

Fig. 69

The later Saxon period saw Viking raids affecting much of Britain. At various times, Mersea, Benfleet and Shoebury were all used as Viking bases. One of the greatest works of early English literature concerns the results of a Viking raid on the Blackwater in the late 11th century. This poem, The Battle of Maldon, is second only in importance to the Beowulf epic, and describes the heroic stand of Byrhtnoth, the earldorman of Essex, against the Norse raiders.

"Can you hear, you pirate, what these people say? They will pay you a tribute of whistling spears, of deadly darts and proven swords, weapons to pay you, pierce, slit and slay you..."

Fig. 69 Maldon (left) This painting depicts the battle of Maldon; the Vikings were based on Northey in the Blackwater estuary and Byrhtnoth and his men were blocking the causeway to the mainland. They bravely and, as it turned out, foolishly pulled back to allow the Vikings to form up on the bank of the Blackwater. In the ensuing battle the English were defeated and Byrhtnoth and many of his men were killed. Compare this picture with the version painted in the 1930s to decorate Braintree Town Hall (Fig 4).

"Mind must be firmer, heart the more fierce, courage the greater as our strength diminishes..."

Fig. 70

Following the Norman Conquest in 1066, probably the most dramatic change to the English landscape was the widespread construction of castles. The huge stone-built keep at Colchester, constructed on the foundations of the temple of Claudius, was begun in 1070 and completed in about 1080. However, most early Norman castles were of earth and timber construction and known as motte and baileys.

These castles comprised a large mound of earth, the motte, which formed the stronghold of the castle. This mound would have been encircled by timber ramparts and might be provided with a central timber tower or keep. Attached to the motte would be one or more courtyards, the baileys, surrounded by banks and ditches. These areas housed most of the domestic structures of the castle.

Fig. 70 Pleshey (above) This air photograph shows Pleshey Castle. The motte is in the centre of the photograph with the bailey, surrounded by its earth bank, beyond and linked to the motte by a late medieval brick bridge. The town was also surrounded by a bank and ditch, much of which still survives and can be seen in the foreground.

There are a number of motte and bailey castles in Essex including particularly fine examples at Pleshey, Chipping Ongar and Rayleigh. Pleshey Castle was built in the early 12th century. Subsequently, a new town was founded by Geoffrey de Mandeville. In the long term, the town did not thrive, being over-shadowed by the nearby, more strategically placed, town founded by the Bishop of London at Chelmsford. As a consequence the major elements of Pleshey's medieval layout survive very well.

Fig. 71

Fig. 73

One of the most important of the Essex motte and baileys is Rayleigh Mount. This castle was built by Swein the sheriff of Essex and Hertfordshire, and was already in existence by the time of the Domesday survey. The earthwork remains of this castle are now a public park in the centre of Rayleigh owned by the National Trust.

Fig. 71 Rayleigh (above) shows the castle as it may have been in the 12th century. The edge of the outer bailey in the foreground of this picture is followed by the present day Bellingham Lane. The inner bailey was separated from the motte by a deep ditch, the motte with a platform half way up was revetted with Kentish Ragstone. These details were revealed by excavations carried out in the 1960s. This picture shows the top of the motte ringed by battlements with a small watchtower, although it is quite possible that a much more substantial timber keep had existed.

A very different form of castle was constructed at Hadleigh. Here the castle is situated on high ground commanding wide views of the Thames estuary, and occupies a defensive position at the end of a spur with the ground dropping sharply away to the east and south. Hadleigh was seized by the crown in 1239. During the 1360s major modifications were made, by order of Edward III to bring the defences up to date and provide suitable accommodation for a royal residence.

Fig. 72

HADLEIGH CASTLE from the west,
reconstruction c. 1250.

Fig. 72 Hadleigh (below left) This picture shows the original castle built by Hurbert de Burgh in the early 13th century. In contrast to the motte and bailey castles Hadleigh was an enclosure castle, a development in military architecture in which the main strength lay in the enclosing walls set with towers rather than a high motte or keep.

Fig. 73 Hadleigh (left) The castle as it may have appeared after Edward III's alterations viewed from the north with the marshes fringing the Thames estuary in the background. This picture clearly shows the new circular towers which replaced most of the earlier rectangular ones, including a magnificent pair of drum towers flanking what had once been the entrance to the castle. Edward III's alterations moved the entrance to the north

side of the castle, protected by an elongated barbican, the gate being flanked by two circular towers. This structure is shown to the right of the picture. In the foreground the large fence is the park pale, which surrounded the deer park attached to the castle.

Fig. 74 Hadleigh (below) This picture shows Hadleigh Castle viewed from the Thames marshes, and displays the castle in its landscape setting, with the deer park separated from the castle by its timber fence, sheep grazing on the slopes, and the dominant position of the castle itself clearly apparent. The wharves in the foreground are conjectural, but documentary sources indicate that great reliance was placed on the Thames for transport of all kinds of goods to and from the castle.

Fig. 74

51

Fig. 75

In contrast to Hadleigh Castle, excavations at King John's Hunting Lodge close to the present day Writtle Agricultural College, have revealed a very different form of royal residence. The main residential part of the site was set on a platform surrounded by a water filled moat. Moated sites are extremely varied and Writtle is one of the most completely excavated and also one of the earliest examples. The site was a royal manor and was well placed to exploit the hunting in the Writtle Forest to the south. The moated site was built by the order of King John in 1211. The manor was generally let to tenants, but rights to use the house and park were retained as royal prerogatives as were rights to hunt in Writtle Forest, and the kings of England were frequent visitors. Throughout the second half of the 13th century the de Bruce family were the tenants until Writtle was forfeited in 1306 because of Robert de Bruce's leading role in opposing Edward I's attempts at the conquest of Scotland.

Fig. 75 Writtle (left) This painting shows the Royal Manor of Writtle during a visit by Edward I and Queen Margaret, which took place in 1305. The main residence is on the moated island with the great hall in the centre; the stone building to the left is the chapel; the building to the right of the hall with smoke rising from it is the kitchen. The gatehouse by the bridge to the right of the picture is shown decked with flags in honour of the King's visit. The ponds on the extreme right of the picture are fishponds, used to supply fresh fish to the household. Brightly coloured pavilions to accommodate the royal retinue are shown pitched in the foreground. An orchard garden lies to the south of the moat, with a stackyard and barns beyond; these were vital components of the site which was the heart of a great farming estate. The huge open fields of the manor's demesne can be seen stretching between two hedges in the background. On the skyline, to the north, the tower of Pleshey Castle can just be glimpsed. For a detailed account of this reconstruction see Hunter 1993.

Moated sites are very characteristic of medieval settlement in Essex, and in the east of England generally. Essex and Suffolk contend with one another

to claim the largest number of moated sites in any English county. At the moated site at Southchurch Hall, in Southend the Hall survives. It was carefully restored in the 1930s, and is now open to the public as a museum. The Hall is set within attractive gardens which include the earthworks of the moated enclosures. The manor of Southchurch was owned by Christchurch Canterbury. From the late 12th to the early 14th century the tenants were the de Southchurch family, powerful local landowners, and it was they who built the moated site at Southchurch. Excavations by the Southend-on Sea and District Historical and Antiquarian Society, of part of the moat and platform have revealed the considerable wealth and sophistication of the site. Its occupants were able to exploit the trading opportunities offered by the proximity of the Thames Estuary to obtain a wide range of imports. The site is also fortunate in having a wide range of surviving documentary evidence.

Fig. 76 Southchurch (below) shows the restored Hall at Southchurch as it is today. In the foreground are the stone-built foundations of the gatehouse and two garderobes revealed by the excavations.

Fig. 76

Fig. 77

Fig. 77 Southchurch (left) This painting shows the moated site looking north as it may have been in its medieval heyday. Only the central hall survives today, excavations have indicated the position of the kitchens which are shown adjacent to the moat in the centre of the picture, linked to the hall by a covered walkway which is referred to in the documentary sources. The gatehouse and associated buildings, whose foundations were revealed in the excavations, can be seen in the background. On the far left of the picture are large barns in an outer courtyard, known from documentary sources and which appear on 18th and 19th century maps, this area is now entirely covered with 20th century housing.

Fig. 78 Southchurch (right) Essex was one of the great centres of the Peasants' Revolt of 1381 and this vivid picture shows Southchurch Hall being attacked during the Revolt. The Hall is shown very much as it was following the restoration of c.1930. The other buildings reflect the information contained in the documentary sources. The picture was painted long before any excavation was carried out at the site and this explains the rather more ramshackle appearance of many of the buildings when compared to the previous painting. The depiction of the gatehouse is of particular interest. This structure is mentioned in the documentary sources. The building shown in this painting is clearly modelled on a gatehouse at Kents, otherwise known as Moat House, in North Shoebury a few miles north-east of Southchurch Hall. The North Shoebury building would have been very much in Sorrell's mind as a model for the appearance of the Southchurch gatehouse. In the early 1930s the owners of Moat House, the Southend Estates Company, suggested a scheme, recorded in the Transactions of the Southend Historical & Antiquarian Society, to dismantle the gatehouse and re-erect it at Southchurch Hall. In the event this scheme came to nothing, and the North Shoebury gatehouse was demolished in the 1960s. The excavations at Southchurch Hall subsequently showed the gatehouse there to have been a much more substantial building, with stone foundations which can be seen in Fig. 76.

Fig. 78

55

Fig. 79

Another manorial centre also open to the public is at Cressing Temple. Owned by Essex County Council, this is renowned for its two magnificent Early Medieval barns. Cressing Temple takes its name from the crusading order of the Knights Templar. The manor of Cressing was the first rural estate granted to the order in England. Of the Templar buildings on the site, only the two great barns survive together with a stone lined well. The best idea of the buildings which would once have accompanied the barns comes from an inventory of 1313. This mentions a chapel two chambers, a hall, a pantry, a buttery, a kitchen, a larder, a bakehouse, a brewhouse, a dairy, a granary and a smithy. Excavations have uncovered the foundations of the chapel, the Hall, and two stone chambers ranged north-south in the space between the present garden and granary.

The Templar estate would have been in the charge of a preceptor accompanied by two or three resident knights or sergeants at arms, together with a chaplain, a bailiff, and numerous household servants. In addition, the estate would have employed agricultural labourers, shepherds, millers, gardeners and craftsmen.

Fig. 79 Cressing (above). This reconstruction shows the site as it may have been c. 1300. It is estimated that by that time Cressing was the centre of a large farming estate. In the right-hand corner of the enclosure are the chapel, hall and two stone chambers. The elongated ponds on the extreme right of the picture are the site's fishponds, like those in the picture of Writtle (Fig 75). The two great barns dominate the centre of the painting.

One of the major influences on medieval life and landscape were the monastic orders and their landholdings. One of the greatest of medieval abbeys was Waltham Abbey. Today only the nave of the Romanesque apse-and-ambulatory church of Holy Cross and St. Lawrence remains as the parish church. It is one of 25 churches of this type known in England; three of these, Gloucester cathedral, Norwich cathedral and the priory church of St. Bartholomew at Smithfield, London, survive as standing churches. The form is typical of pilgrimage churches which allow the efficient circulation of people up one aisle to places of special devotion, on round the apse at the east end and back down the other aisle. At Waltham there were a number of relics but the chief object of devotion was the wonder working Holy Cross. This was a crucifix said to have been found at Montacute, Somerset and brought to Waltham in about 1030 in the reign of King Canute.

Excavations by Waltham Abbey Historical Society mainly between 1984 and 1991, have revealed the plans of five successive churches. The first was a simple timber building which is currently dated to the bishopric of Mellitus, 604-616AD. The second was a stone church dated to about 790AD. The third was built by Harold (who later became king and was killed at the battle of Hastings) and dedicated in 1060AD. Harold's church was of a somewhat old-fashioned form when first built, and after the Norman Conquest was replaced by a fashionable Norman style church, which is shown in the reconstructions reproduced here, and probably took about 50 years to build. Towards the end of the twelfth century, this church was itself remodelled.

In order to produce the computer generated reconstruction pictures of the Norman church shown here the Waltham Abbey Historical Society produced drawings of the plan, and reconstructed various sections through the church from which the artist John Carter worked. Many decisions had to be made based on existing evidence and on consideration of parallels from other churches. The early Romanesque architectural style in England has much in common with the style across the Channel. The church at Jumièges, in France, begun in 1040, is the best known predecessor of the English churches.

The Waltham church is relatively narrow for a building of its type, this is because the width was determined by the re-use of the foundations of the previous church. Comparison with a French church at Notre-dame du Port at Clermont Ferrand, with its solid apse columns, was crucial to the interpretation of the Waltham Church. The narrow width of the church meant that there was only room for relatively small diameter columns which therefore had to be solid drums rather than rubble-filled columns such as those that remain in the nave. Today there is a central western tower built c.1556. The two westernmost piers show that they originally supported twin western towers and detailed study of the fabric outside shows that one corner of these slightly projecting towers

remains. In the reconstruction, the design of these towers and of the central tower is based on the churches at Southwell, Nottinghamshire and Tewkesbury in Gloucestershire respectively. The design of the western front with its three doors and sets of windows is based on Durham cathedral and a church at Bosherville in the Seine valley.

Around the outside of the east end of the church, evidence of two of a set of three 'bubble' chapels, added probably in the 1120s, was found in the excavations. The easternmost chapel, which can be glimpsed in the internal view, is thought to have been a new setting for the Holy Cross. The wooden screen in the internal view is based on a 12th century example from Surrey. The nave altar is conjectural but there is some indication that there was an altar there in the 14th century. The door in the south transept is based on that at Southwell; the southern door in the nave still exists at Waltham Abbey and was the model for the three western doors. The south door is wrongly shown in a bay too far east but this was not spotted until the work was too far advanced to correct, an indication of the many difficulties which beset reconstruction work. The nave in the internal view is much as it is today, however the aisles are shown paved at gallery level. The gallery itself would have been lit by the bulls-eye windows. There is some evidence that the aisles were covered with intersecting barrel vaulting. No attempt has been made to show the brightly coloured wall paintings which would have decorated the interior.

Fig. 80 Waltham Abbey (below). View of the church seen from the south west, showing the twin western towers and the central bell tower. Beyond the south transept can be seen one of the three 'bubble' chapels.

Fig. 81 Waltham Abbey (below). Internal view of the Norman church from the west, beyond the nave and the chancel arches can be seen the solid drum apse columns, between the central columns can be seen the altar in the added eastern chapel.

Fig. 82 Waltham Abbey (right) Internal view of the Norman church looking up to the floor of the ringing chamber in the central tower, to the left looking up into the roof of the south transept, to the right looking through the nave arch at the nave roof structure.

Fig. 83 Barking (next page) This picture by the architect Sir Charles Nicholson, of Barking Abbey looking south shows the extremely complex and extensive layout of a great monastery in its heyday. In the foreground are the chimneys of the kitchens and bakehouse linked by a covered passage to the refectory or dining hall forming the north side of the cloisters. The centre of the picture is dominated by the great abbey church. Beyond the west end of the church, on the right of the picture, is the well appointed house of the abbess. Behind the abbey church can be seen the smaller parish church of St. Margaret which still survives, and outside the abbey's precinct wall the small thriving town of Barking, then a major fishing port. In the top right corner is the large abbey mill, powered by the waters of Barking creek.

Fig. 83

*Fig. 84 **Prittlewell** (below). This picture shows the much smaller site of Prittlewell Priory, again shortly before its dissolution. Today the site lies within Priory Park in Southend. Substantial parts of the buildings in the foreground of this picture survive, and are open to the public. The foundations of the church can also be seen. Not shown in this picture are the priory's fishponds which still survive and lie just beyond the right-hand edge of the picture. The apparent parkland setting may reflect more the 20th century appearance of Priory Park than the late medieval landscape.*

*Fig. 85 **Colchester** (right) This picture shows the magnificent west front of St. Botolph's Priory church as it may have been in about 1200. The Priory was largely destroyed during the siege of Colchester in 1648. The ruins still convey a good impression of the original magnificence of the church.*

Fig. 85

Fig. 86

Fig. 86 Colchester (above) Of the towns of medieval Essex, Colchester was the largest and most important. This painting shows the town as it may have been in about 1150, surrounded by the Roman walls and dominated by the castle built on the foundations of the Temple of Claudius. St Botolph's Priory is on the right of the picture just outside the town walls, with St. John's Abbey in the foreground in the bottom right hand corner of the picture.

One of the great glories of Essex is its wealth of ancient timber framed buildings, which can tell us much about the county's medieval towns. These two pages depict reconstructions by Dave Stenning and Cecil Hewett of some of the finest examples in Essex towns.

Reconstruction drawings of historical buildings are a fascinating exercise in that they can suggest a view into the past but they can have the capacity to mislead if not based on scrupulous research. Suitable subjects are thus relatively rare - all reconstructions will be 'wrong' to some degree, but sufficient evidence ought to be available in order to provide a reasonable interpretation.

Fig. 88. The well known authority on timber framed buildings, the late Cecil Hewett, also produced a reconstruction of Thaxted Guildhall. He was able to incorporate knowledge gained during an extensive restoration project, where much of the structure was revealed. Nevertheless, this drawing has rather more informed speculation than Hewett would normally have allowed himself to contemplate.

*Fig. 87 **Thaxted** (above) Stoney Lane, Thaxted offers one such tempting subject with its impressive range of late medieval buildings. This group of merchants' houses represents 'market-infill' on the recognised classic pattern. All but one of the units has had its later coat of render removed, a condition that has provoked some adverse comment. However, intriguing remnants of the frames are revealed, allowing their original appearance to be reasonably discerned and illustrated in this picture. There is substantial evidence for ground-floor shops, but where and how access was gained to the cellars underneath remains a question. This particular illustration incorporates a blank area where the detailed nature of the building remains unknown. Perhaps in the future it will be possible to fill in the blanks if more information comes to light. To the left of the illustration, part of Thaxted Guildhall appears.*

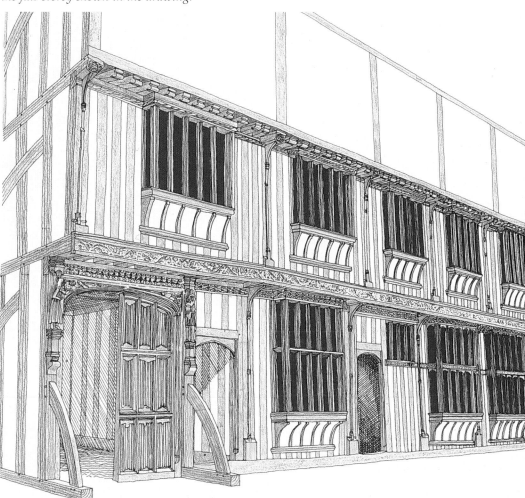

Fig. 90 Coggeshall (below) The well-known Paycockes House at Coggeshall shown in the picture introduces another factor. This elaborate wool merchant's house of the early 16th century is, in part, already a reconstruction. Much of the exterior dates from the early years of the 20th century, but this appears to be a reliable restoration. However, this reconstruction picture takes the process a step further following recent re-evaluation of the evidence. Adjustments have been made to some door and window positions which had been functionally, rather than archaeologically, determined. That Paycockes House was intended to have a third floor (it now has two storeys) can readily be ascertained. Further consideration suggests a low, attic-like third floor may have existed, rather than the full-storey shown in the drawing.

Fig. 89 Brentwood (above) The White Hart, Brentwood incorporates what is arguably the finest 15th century inn range surviving in England. Only part of the structure is shown in that this jettied building abutted a range on the street frontage to the left, and a similar 16th century extension to the right. The building contains two chambers on the first floor, with a continuous open gallery accessed by the staircase at the end (not shown). The ground floor was probably more utilitarian, but too little survives to allow a detailed reconstruction.

Fig. 91 Braintree (above) Very different from Colchester (Fig 86) but more typical of medieval Essex towns was Braintree. This picture shows the original market place as it may have appeared toward the end of the medieval period. The viewer is standing at the southern end of Drury Lane looking north-west across part of the market place. The timber-framed building at the top right hand side of the picture is now the Swan public house. The building in the centre of the picture is a public building, possibly a guildhall, which we know once stood on this site. Nothing of this building now remains and this picture is based on similar buildings from elsewhere in the county. To the left, a group of permanent market stalls are shown.

The church formed a major focus of medieval settlements, both urban and rural. In Essex, medieval rural settlement was generally dispersed, church/hall complexes forming focal points. There are of course numerous exceptions to this general rule, one of which is the church at Prittlewell which lay at the heart of a nucleated village.

*Fig. 92 Prittlewell (right). Prittlewell is one of the largest churches in south Essex and this picture shows the construction of the tower in the mid 15th century. The two houses shown on the left of the picture are late medieval buildings which survive to this day on the west side of Victoria Avenue (formerly North Street). Prittlewell Priory can just be seen in the background on the upper right of the picture. The depiction of the churchyard is of some interest, the street frontage is shown without buildings as it largely is today. In contrast, the Chapman and Andre map of 1777 shows the church-yard lined with buildings facing North Street and East Street, with the church behind, rather like the present day situation of the churchyard at, for instance, Chelmsford. It seems likely that by the late medieval period, the churchyard at Prittlewell would already have been surrounded by buildings. However, a long campaign by Canon Gowing, the Vicar of Prittlewell in the early 20th century, to remove buildings around the churchyard and restore it to what he regarded as its original medieval appearance, had by the 1930s largely succeeded, aided by the need to widen Victoria Avenue.
The open appearance of the churchyard is therefore more likely to reflect the 'politically correct' view of the 1930s rather than the later medieval reality.*

Fig. 92

Fig. 93

Fig. 93 Stebbingford This medieval farm was located on the crest of the slope on the east side of the Stebbing Brook Valley, and was excavated prior to construction of the new A120. This reconstruction represents the farmstead between about 1200-1270 AD, looking north-east. The largest of the three buildings was interpreted as a kitchen/dwelling-house on the basis of its two internal hearths/ovens. In front of it was a smaller building, internally sub-divided into two very small rooms. This may have been another dwelling-house or a store. The midden area and cess-pits backed on to this building. To the rear of these buildings was a long, thin open-sided structure, interpreted as a byre on the basis of comparison with surviving late medieval structures and illustrations in manuscripts. In front of the byre was a small pond and behind an enclosed yard (where the haystacks are depicted). The buildings were sited on a level promontory, and the ground dropped steeply both to the west and south. To the south was a small spring-fed stream, very peaty and marshy along its banks. The south-facing slope above it had a very sandy subsoil and appears to have been the location of the farmstead's garden. A number of beds had been dug during the medieval period and filled with a mix of peat from the stream's edge and waste from the midden area. The remainder of the farm was laid out in a regular pattern of long strip-fields, at right-angles to Stane Street, the main road to Dunmow, Braintree and Colchester (the A120) which is visible in the middle distance of the illustration.

Extensive excavations over the last 15 years or so have revealed a range of medieval rural farmsteads. Most notable of these is at Stebbingford where the complete plan of a medieval settlement was recorded during excavations in advance of construction of the new A120 (previous page).

Fig. 94 Boreham A somewhat different medieval farming complex has been excavated at Boreham in advance of gravel extraction. Here, remains of buildings, including a possible granary were found set within an area of ditched enclosures and fields. In one corner a circular feature may have been the site of a windmill. The mill shown here is based on examples in medieval illustrations.

Following the dissolution of the monasteries in the mid 16th century, many of the main monastic properties were converted into the residences of prominent secular families. Cressing Temple was sold to Sir John Smyth by Henry VIII. By the late 16th century a brick mansion had been constructed as a family seat though nothing of it stands today.

Fig. 95 Cressing (above) This painting shows Cressing Temple as it may have appeared in about 1630. The great medieval barns and chapel survive from the earlier layout with the new house built around a courtyard; excavations have revealed its cellars and drains. The main approach is shown flanked by ranges of agricultural buildings, that in the background on the right-hand side of the picture still survives at the site today. The garden, surrounded by a brick wall of 16th century date, and shown in this painting adjoining the house, has recently been laid out and replanted in the style of the 16th century.

Fig. 96 Gestingthorpe (right) Construction of the tower of Gestingthorpe church in the 1520s. By the 16th century brick was a highly fashionable building material, and Essex was at the forefront of brick manufacture and building. The picture shows the priest and local gentry discussing the building with workmen mixing mortar and unloading bricks close to the tower, which is nearing completion. The bricks would have been made locally. This picture was the first undertaken by Benjamin Perkins to illustrate the work of the local historian Ashley Cooper.

8. The Post-Medieval Period

67

Fig. 97

68

Fig. 97 Chelmsford (left) This picture shows Chelmsford High Street looking north towards the church in the late 16th century. The broad triangular space in front of the church was then the market place. The wedge of buildings in the centre were originally market stalls which had become permanent buildings. This wedge can still be seen today as the buildings which separate High Street from Tindal Street. This picture is based on one of the maps drawn up by the Walkers of Hanningfield, a father and son partnership who produced many accurate estate maps in the late 16th and early 17th centuries (Edwards and Newton 1984). The layout of the town together with fields and trees can therefore be regarded as good representations of what actually existed over four hundred years ago.

Fig. 98 Thorndon Old Hall (above) In 1573 John Petre bought a large 15th century brick house at West Horndon and over the next twenty years set about a major rebuilding programme that transformed it into a classic Elizabethan mansion as shown in this painting. The house was 270 feet long with multiple gables, towers and tall, ornate chimneys. The many large windows afforded fine views over Petre's large estates across the south Essex plain towards the Thames estuary. Fashionable though they might be, all these windows did not necessarily make for comfort. Writing of this fashion, Francis Bacon commented "You shall sometimes have fair houses so full of glass, that one cannot tell where to become out of the sun or cold". The house was demolished in the mid-18th century but appears on one of the Walker maps and detailed building accounts survive. These and other sources have been used to guide this reconstruction, which gives a good idea of how impressive this great house must have been at the end of the 16th century.

The extremely long Essex coastline made the area vulnerable to invasion in time of war. Throughout the second half of the 17th century trading rivalry between England and the Netherlands led to a series of wars. In the 1650s following the defeat of the Royalists in the civil wars of the 1640s and the execution of the king, the new republic's navy under Admiral Blake successfully defeated the Dutch. Leigh, today the western most part of Southend, but then a thriving port, was used by Blake as a base for supplying and refitting the fleet anchored in the Nore.

Fig. 99 Leigh (left) This picture, the first historical reconstruction ever undertaken by Alan Sorrell, shows in the foreground boats being loaded to take supplies, messages and personnel to and from the fleet anchored in the estuary. In the middle distance one of the ships has been heeled over to facilitate repairs below the waterline. The meticulous detail of the shipping and dress are the result of painstaking research described by Sorrel in a contemporary article (Sorrell 1934).

Following the restoration of the monarchy the English navy failed to maintain its earlier success against the Dutch, and in 1667 the Dutch fleet entered the Thames estuary and destroyed many ships in the Medway. Samuel Pepys, MP for Harwich and a navy official, sadly noted in his diary the poor performance of the Navy compared with its success in Cromwell's time,"...*our Ambassadors are treating at Breda and the Dutch look upon them as come to beg peace, and use them accordingly. And all this through the negligence of our Prince; who hath power, if he would, to master all these with money and men that he hath had command of, and may now have if he would mind his business. But for aught we see, the Kingdom is likely to be lost, as well as the reputation of it is, for ever - notwithstanding so much reputation got and preserved by a Rebell that went before him."*

The shock of the Dutch success led to an improvement to the defences of the Thames, including the construction of an elaborate fort at Tilbury, built to the design of Sir Bernard de Gomme the eminent military engineer.

Fig. 100 Tilbury (right) This aerial photograph shows the elaborate geometry of Tilbury Fort and the restored drawbridges. The Fort is now in the guardianship of English Heritage and is open to the public.

Fig. 102 Tilbury Fort (below)
The monumental 17th century
Water Gate designed in Sir
Christopher Wren's office.

Fig. 101 Tilbury (above) This painting shows the fort as it may have appeared in the 19th century, with massive batteries facing the Thames, and docks and jetties giving access to the Water Gate from the river. The land approach entered the fort through a series of redoubts and crossed the moat and ditches by means of draw-bridges shown in the background of this painting. Inside the fort is a parade ground and 18th century barrack blocks. The weather boarded building in the foreground is the World's End Pub.

A major threat of invasion came during the Napoleonic wars. Between 1808 and 1812, a chain of small forts called Martello towers, was built on the Essex and Suffolk coasts from St. Osyth to Aldeburgh. They were named after a tower on Martella Point in Corsica which with only three guns repulsed two British ships armed with 106 guns. The Essex towers were about 30ft high, built in brick later covered in stucco.

Fig. 103 Walton (left). This painting shows a Martello tower at Walton-on-the-Naze placed to defend the town hard with its windmill on the left and tidemill on the right of the picture. The tower was ovoid in plan with the sea facing walls about 13 feet thick and the inland wall about 5 feet thick. The entrance to the tower was on the first floor approached by a ladder. The armament consisted of three 24-pounder guns, mounted on the roof.

Fig. 104 Harwich (above) Bathside Bay Battery - detail of one of the gun positions, also of Napoleonic date. Important though these shore-based fortifications were considered to be, the first line of defence was the navy, and Harwich was a major naval base.

Fig. 105 Harwich (right) This computer-generated image shows the Bathside Bay defences. These comprised a brick built D-shaped structure with three cannon mounted on gun platforms; the rear of the battery was closed by a wooden fence.

Fig. 106 Harwich (left) Amongst the most notable of the defences at Harwich was the redoubt. This painting shows it as it would have appeared in its early 19th century heyday. It was a circular fort built between 1807 and 1810, and was 200 feet in diameter with walls over 8 feet thick surrounded by a deep moat. Ten 24-pounder guns were mounted on the roof. The interior was occupied by a circular parade ground, surrounded by heavily protected chambers known as casemates which housed the garrison and its stores.

Fig. 108 Harwich (below) This panoramic view of Harwich at the beginning of the 19th century is based on contemporary sketches thought to have been made by a serviceman stationed at Harwich. It shows the numerous naval and other vessels in the estuary, and the compact nature of the town at this time. The buildings in the foreground are military structures comprising officers' quarters, stores, an armoury and a magazine.

Fig. 107 Harwich (left) Harwich redoubt as it is today seen from the air. The houses and road in the foreground are on reclaimed land and the fort is now surrounded by an intriguing patchwork of allotments. The brick and concrete structures on the roof relate to use of the redoubt during the Second World War.

In the mid 19th century new developments in naval construction and in the effectiveness of artillery led to a kind of arms race and renewed invasion scares. In 1859 a Royal Commission on the Defence of the United Kingdom was set up which, when it reported in 1860, proposed a defensive scheme more expensive than any earlier attempts. Improvements to artillery meant that new forts had to be built to defend the Thames estuary effectively. This was achieved by constructing a pair of forts at Shornemead in Kent and Coalhouse in Essex, about three miles east of Tilbury Fort, commanding Lower Hope Reach. Construction at Coalhouse began in 1861, but owing to design changes was not completed until 1874, the final phase of construction being supervised by Charles Gordon, later to become famous as Gordon of Khartoum.

Fig 109 Tilbury (left) Coalhouse Fort is one of the finest remaining examples of an armoured casemate fort in the country. This picture shows the fort as it probably looked when originally built. It consisted of a curved battery of granite faced casemates, protected by a thick vaulted roof of concrete and brick. There was an open battery at the up river end. The barrack blocks shown closing off the rear of the fort in the picture were built of Kentish Ragstone and were provided with loopholes for defence against attack from the landward side. The Thames barges shown in the background were used for transporting goods around the Essex coast throughout the 19th and early 20th centuries.

Fig. 110 Tilbury (above) This air photograph shows Coalhouse Fort as it is today set in a public park. The curving arc of the defensive moat is a marked contrast to the angular pattern of the Tilbury Fort reflecting the changing nature of defensive requirements.

The defences at Harwich were not improved in the mid 19th century. In 1887 a report by the Inspector-General of Fortifications stated that Harwich had become the weakest point in the country's defences. In response to this a new fort was built at Beacon Hill to the south of the town, and equipped with the most modern breech-loading guns on disappearing mountings. The defences at Beacon Hill were continually updated. The fort remained in use through both the World Wars of the 20th century, and into the post-war period.

Fig. 111 Harwich (above) This painting shows the site as it may have been just after World War II, with anti-aircraft guns and other ordnance scattered around the site, and considerable evidence of earlier gun emplacements and other installations no longer in use. In the background two military vehicles are shown turning into the site from Barrack Lane.

Apart from the threat of invasion the coastline offered more peaceful attractions; with the fashion for sea bathing Southend began to be developed as a seaside resort. The Royal Terrace on the clifftop was the core of the new development. An autumn spent at Southend is famously described in Jane Austen's 'Emma' by Mrs. John Knightly "We all had our health perfectly there" and "never found the least inconvenience from the mud".

Fig. 112 Southend (right) Here the first mail coach to arrive at the new resort of Southend is shown at the top of what is now known as Pier Hill. The buildings on the left have been demolished but the Royal Terrace itself, seen stretching along the clifftop in the middle distance, survives looking much as it does in this painting. Compare this finished picture with Sorrell's much smaller oil sketch (Fig 1).

At the end of the 18th century and beginning of the 19th century East Anglia was at the forefront of the Agricultural Revolution. Many new crops and farming techniques were developed and many Essex farmers played an active role in these developments, many of which were recorded by the famous agrarian writer Arthur Young.

Fig. 113 Little Maplestead (below) depicts a scene in about 1800 and shows the agricultural improver John Sewell of Little Maplestead Hall watching a 'mole drainer'

which he had built in co-operation with a Mr. Vaizey of Halstead. The tremendous number of horses harnessed together pulled an iron bullet or 'mole' at a depth of 14-18 inches through the subsoil. This created a tunnel about two inches wide through the clay to improve drainage. In the background can be seen Little Maplestead church, then rather dilapidated, with an elongated timber framed porch but without dormer windows. In 1807 Arthur Young published a diagram of Sewell and Vaisey's mole drainer on which this picture is based (Cooper 1998 XXVII)

Fig. 114 Castle Hedingham (left) Another very active agricultural improver at this time was Lewis Majendie who owned Hedingham Castle. He adopted the remarkably advanced practice of sowing particular types of grass for pasture, rather than the random mix of grass and weed seeds used at the time. Majendie also introduced Dutch White Clover into north-east Essex. In 1786 he adopted the use of the seed drill, using a machine designed by Rev. James Cooke of Lancashire. Here Majendie is shown discussing his seed drill with another keen local agricuturalist, Mrs. Clarke of Lawrence's Farm. Hedingham Castle can be seen in the background. To the left of the picture are two of the grasses which Majendie investigated, Meadow Foxtail, and Meadow Fescue, with White Clover on the bottom right and a hop bine above. The Hedinghams had a great reputation for hop growing at the time (Cooper 1998).

Fig. 115 Hylands House (right) Essex has long been a favoured location for the country residences of the wealthy (see Figs 95 and 98 for 16th century examples). This picture shows the neo-classical entrance hall of Hylands House, Chelmsford, owned from 1815 to 1839 by Pierre Labouchere, a Dutch Hugenot and merchant banker. Labouchere was a patron of the Danish sculptor, Bertel Thorvaldsen, and commissioned the Venus (now in the Thorvaldsen Museum, Copenhagen) and the bust of his son, Henry. The plaster reliefs of 'Dawn' and 'Night' are still in situ. The entrance hall was restored by Chelmsford Borough Council in 1995.

81

At the end of the 19th and beginning of the 20th century, agricultural depression meant that many Essex farms were semi-derelict or derelict and abandoned, particularly on the heavy claylands of south and east Essex. Enterprising entrepreneurs bought up these farms at rock bottom prices, and split them up into individual plots to be sold separately. Advertised as an opportunity to live in an arcadian paradise, the sales were often promoted by means of free or cheap train excursions to view the sites, accompanied by free food and drink on arrival. These 'Plotlands' proved very attractive to people living in cramped east end slum conditions, but they brought many problems and already in 1898 the plotland dwellers were being described as 'squatters' whose style of living "might do in the Australian bush or the American backwoods but it is hardly what one might expect in the highly civilised county of Essex" (Frankland 1992). The high point of plotland development was the period between the First and Second World Wars. There was a major concentration of plotland settlements in the Basildon area.

Many former plotland inhabitants have fond memories of their former homes and there is no doubt that the pleasant rolling countryside of Basildon District, overlooking the broad estuary of the Thames, was an attractive proposition to someone living in a crowded London street. But by the late 1940s the problems of this kind of development were enormous. A report in the 'News Chronicle' for January 3rd 1947 describes 40,000 people living in what is now Basildon with "unmade streets as deep in mire as a medieval cattle track". So bad were the roads that coal or other heavy loads could only be delivered in summer when the roads were dry. The News Chronicle reporter took as an example "a square mile of Laindon. Within it there are 923 dwellings of every sort, practically all on unmade roads, without water, electric light, sewage. Gas reaches out to possibly half of them. They are built of wood, asbestos and a few of brick." The reporter goes on to describe in detail the living conditions of one family, "All the slops, including the contents of the sanitation pail, go into the 'garden'. Not unnaturally, the garden well is fit neither for drinking nor washing, and therefore all the water must be brought in buckets from a standpipe five minutes away." The new town of Basildon was designed and built to replace these ramshackle dwellings and bring modern living conditions to their inhabitants.

Fig. 116 Basildon (below) A typical plotland as it may have looked in about 1930. The artist has depicted a summer's day just after a heavy thunder storm which is shown moving away on the right of the picture. This allows the painting to demonstrate how attractive the plotlands could appear in bright summer weather, but also to indicate some of the draw backs. The car in the centre of the picture has become stuck in a muddy rut following the heavy rain. The picture also shows the variety of buildings and building materials, vacant plots some plots with well tended gardens others rather overgrown. Note also the verandah and sunburst gate and fence of the building in the left foreground, typical features of the period.

9. Picturing the Future

Fig. 117. This painting shows the building of a new approach to the centre of Southend in the mid 1960s, and no doubt is the kind of picture Alan Sorrell originally hoped to paint when he first approached Southend Borough Council 30 years earlier. The viewpoint is from the top of the new Civic Centre, looking down on the construction of the Court House. At this time some of the rather grand late 19th century houses which once lined Victoria Avenue still survived. These have now gone to be replaced by the tower blocks which give the road its present, striking, somewhat Chicago-esque, appearance. It is reminiscent of that mid-western city not only in terms of the size of the buildings, but in the strength of the wind which blows around them. The red brick, slate-roofed building behind the bowling green in the centre of the picture is the library building which originally housed Sorrell's 1930s paintings. This now serves as Southend Central Museum.

83

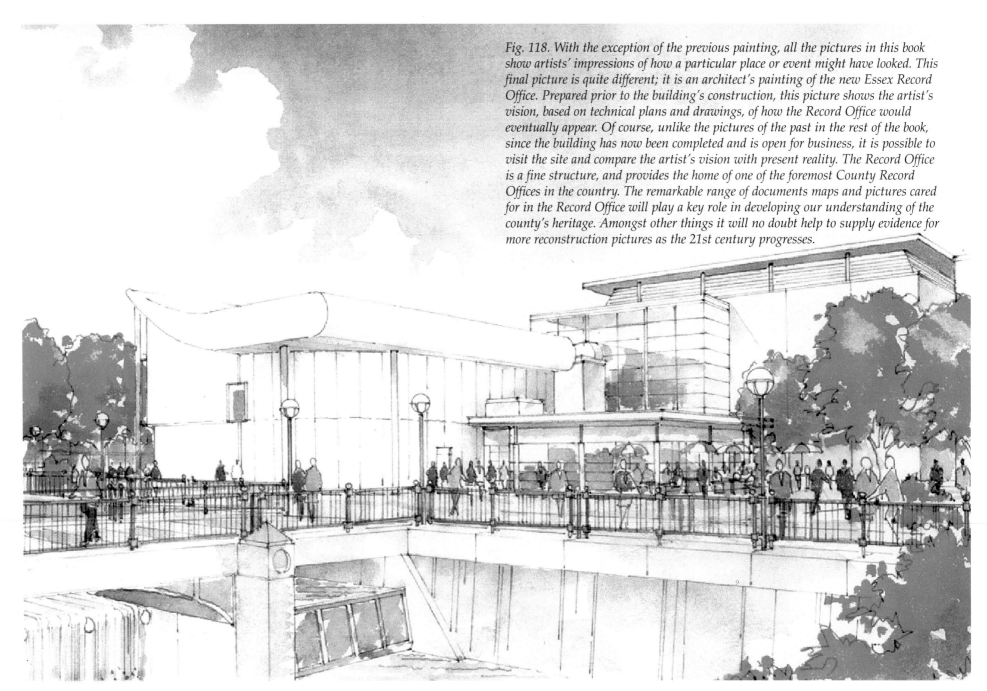

Fig. 118. With the exception of the previous painting, all the pictures in this book show artists' impressions of how a particular place or event might have looked. This final picture is quite different; it is an architect's painting of the new Essex Record Office. Prepared prior to the building's construction, this picture shows the artist's vision, based on technical plans and drawings, of how the Record Office would eventually appear. Of course, unlike the pictures of the past in the rest of the book, since the building has now been completed and is open for business, it is possible to visit the site and compare the artist's vision with present reality. The Record Office is a fine structure, and provides the home of one of the foremost County Record Offices in the country. The remarkable range of documents maps and pictures cared for in the Record Office will play a key role in developing our understanding of the county's heritage. Amongst other things it will no doubt help to supply evidence for more reconstruction pictures as the 21st century progresses.

Bibliography

Bedwin, O.	1996	*The archaeology of Essex; proceedings of the Writtle Conference*
Brown, N.	2000	*The Archaeology of Ardleigh, Essex: Excavations 1955-1980* East Anglian Archaeology
Cooper, A.	1994	*Heart of our history*
Cooper, A.	1998	*Our Mother Earth*
Courtauld, W. J.	1931	*A short description of the pictures and bells, in the Town Hall, Braintree*
Crummy, P.	1997	*City of Victory - the story of Colchester, Britain's first Roman town*
Edwards, A.C. and Newton, K.C.	1984	*The Walkers of Hanningfield*
Essex County Council	1939	*The Council Chamber of the Essex County Council: an account of the decoration the gift of C. W. J. Courtauld*
Essex County Council	1947	*Wall Paintings in the Council Chamber and lobby of the County Hall*
Essex Record Office	1997	*Essex illustrated - a County, its People and its Past*
Frankland, J.	1992	*South Woodham Ferrers: a pictorial history*
Gurney-Benham, W.	1933	'Grant of Arms to the Essex County Council' *Transactions of the Southend-on-Sea Antiquarian and Historical Society*, 2 No.3, 183-188
Havis, R.	1993	'Roman Braintree : excavations 1984-90' *Essex Archaeology and History* 24, 22-68
Helliwell, L. and Macleod, D.G.	1981	*Rayleigh Castle*
Hunter, J.	1993	'King John's Hunting Lodge at Writtle', *Essex Archaeology and History*, 24, 122-4
Hunter, J.	1999	*The Essex Landscape: a study of its form and history*
Johnston, P.	1921-22	'Prittlewell Priory' *Transactions of the Southend-on-Sea Antiquarian and Historical Society* Vol. 1, Part 1, 13-49
MacCarthy, F.	1994	*William Morris: a life for our time*
Marriage, J.	1994	*Braintree and Bocking: a pictorial history*
Medlycott, M.	1999	*Origins of Braintree*
Piggott, S.	1989	*Ancient Britons and the Antiquarian Imagination*
Pollitt, W.	1935	'The Archaeology of Rochford Hundred and south-east Essex' *Transactions of the Southend-on-Sea Antiquarian and Historical Society* Vol. 3, No. 1, 12-63
Sorrell, A.	1934	'The Mural Paintings for the Central Library, Southend-on-Sea' *Transactions of the Southend-on-Sea Antiquarian and Historical Society* Vol. 2, No. 4, 263-269
Sorrell, M. ed.	1981	*Alan Sorrell: Reconstructing the past*

Further reading

Accounts of the latest archaeological and historical investigations in Essex appear in 'Essex Archaeology and History', the annual journal of the Essex Society for Archaeology and History. It is also worth looking out for Essex County Council's annual newspaper supplement 'Essex Past and Present', issued free with the 'Essex Chronicle' each November, and subsequently available from the main museums and libraries in the county.

'The Archaeology of Essex' edited by Owen Bedwin, provides the most up to date summary of Essex archaeology at an academic level. Davy Strachan's 'Essex from the Air' views the county's past through the medium of aerial photography. Two recent publications, 'The Essex Landscape: in Search of its History' edited by Sarah Green, and 'The Essex Landscape: a Study of its Form and History" by John Hunter, provide well illustrated insights into the development of the county's varied landscape. The quotations from the Battle of Maldon (page 48) are taken from K. Crossley - Holland's translation in 'The Anglo Saxon World: an anthology'.

A series of booklets on historic towns in Essex provides accessible accounts of particular towns, incorporating many reconstruction pictures and sketches. Details of many of these publications can be obtained from Roger Massey-Ryan of Essex County Council, Heritage Conservation, Planning Division, County Hall, Chelmsford. Telephone: 01245 437633

In addition, 'City of Victory' by Philip Crummy, a history of Roman and Medieval Colchester, is illustrated with many reconstruction pictures. The books of Ashley Cooper, particularly the two listed in the bibliography, have many reconstruction pictures mainly of the rural past of the north of the county.

Places to visit

Many reconstruction pictures and pictures and paintings can be seen incorporated in the displays at museums. Some examples follow; it is by no means an exhaustive list but provides a selection of examples from around the County. It is likely that your local museum also has reconstruction pictures and paintings incorporated in its displays. Saffron Walden Museum has finds from the excavations carried out at Stansted airport including those sites represented in this book. Colchester Museum, in Colchester Castle, has fine displays on the archaeology of north-east Essex in general, and Colchester in particular. Chelmsford Museum has, amongst other reconstructions, the picture of Chelmsford market place in 1590 (Fig. 97) as part of its displays covering the archaeology of the County town and surrounding area. Valence House Museum, Dagenham, itself an interesting historic building, houses the fine picture of Barking Abbey (Fig. 83) in its late medieval heyday.

The museums in Southend are home to a number of Alan Sorrell's paintings, the four original pictures he painted for the Library are now displayed in the Prittlewell Priory Museum. His picture of Southchurch Hall can be seen in the hall building, the interior of which has been laid out as it might have appeared in the late medieval period.

It is possible to visit many of the sites depicted in the paintings, and some suggestions for a few places to visit are given below. Tourist Information Centres and the annual brochure 'Places to Visit in Essex' will suggest many more. Both Coalhouse and Tilbury forts are open to the public. The earthworks of Rayleigh castle, form a public open space owned by the National Trust.

The magnificent barns at Cressing Temple, depicted at two points in their long history in the paintings shown on pages 79 and 95, are now owned by the County Council and are also open to the public. At Cressing you can go one step further than looking at a reconstruction painting and walk through a living reconstruction of a 16th century walled garden, set within the original Tudor brick garden walls. The dramatic ruins of Hadleigh Castle commanding fine views across the Thames estuary are set within a Country Park which offers good opportunities to explore Hadleigh downs and the marshes fringing Benfleet Creek. The site of Thorndon Old Hall lies within the extensive Thorndon Country Park, where informed by the displays in the visitor centre, it is possible to explore a large area of ancient landscape, some of which is contemporary with Thorndon Old Hall, other elements being far older.

Acknowledgements

In many ways this book represents a collective effort, a remarkable number of individuals and institutions have generously provided help, advice, and permission to reproduce pictures. Almost all the staff of Essex County Council's Heritage Conservation Branch have assisted in one way or another, in particular David Andrews, Dave Stenning and Roger Massey-Ryan have provided much help advice and comment. Pete Rogers and Keith Page kindly provided numerous photographic prints and transparencies often at short notice. Terry Staplehurst and Dave Scrutton were responsible for designing the book and guiding it through the printers.

Southend Borough Council's Museum Service has provided much assistance; the staff of the Central Museum, Prittlewell Priory, Southchurch Hall and Beecroft Art Gallery have all provided help during frequent visits, and Figs. 1, 2, 72, 77, 78, 92, 99 and 112 are reproduced by permission of Southend Borough Council. Colchester Museum staff, and Colchester Archaeological Trust, Philip Crummy, in particular, provided much help with regard to the many reconstructions of Colchester. Braintree District Council allowed reproduction of figs 3-9. Jon Cotton of the Museum of London facilitated the inclusion of the picture of Uphall Camp and Mark Watson from the Valence House museum arranged for the inclusion of the picture of Barking Abbey.

Janet Smith of the Essex Record Office provided the architect's picture of the Record Office. English Heritage kindly supplied copies of Figs. 34 and 63. Mrs. Lewis allowed reproduction of Fig. 71.

Ashley Cooper, who retains copyright of Figs. 96, 113 and 114, was particularly helpful in not only allowing the inclusion of a number of pictures but also providing the text to go with them. Similarly Peter Huggins of the Waltham Abbey Historical Society provided the pictures of Waltham Abbey and the background information to go with them. Last but by no means least are the artists themselves, they are listed below with relevant figure references.

Sheila Appleton	Fig. 117
Lilias August	Fig. 115
Iain Bell	Fig. 69
John Carter	Fig. 80, 81, 82
Leslie Monk	Fig. 52
Stephen Crummy	Fig. 42
Peter Dunn	Fig. 34
Peter Froste	Fig. 41, 43, 44, 45, 46, 47, 48, 49, 50, 51, 57, 60, 65, 85, 86, 93, 116
Frank Gardiner	Fig. 16, 17, 31, 37, 39, 40, 54, 55, 56, 59, 68, 73, 74, 75, 79, 95, 98, 101, 103, 106, 108, 109, 111

Cecil Hewitt   *Fig. 88*
Roger Massey-Ryan *Fig. 22, 23, 25, 26, 29, 33, 66, 91, 97, 104*
Nick Nethercoat   *Fig. 21, 35, 53, 61*
Charles Nicholson *Fig. 83, 84*
Ruth Parkin   *Fig. 67*
Benjamin Perkins *Fig. 96, 113, 114 (Frontispiece)*
Alan Sorrell   *Fig. 1, 2, 71, 78, 92, 99, 112*
Dave Stenning   *Fig. 87, 89, 90*
George Taylor   *Fig. 63*
Colin Thom   *Fig. 118*
Alec Wade   *Fig. 38, 94, 105*
Arthur Wright   *Fig. 72, 77*

Artists' addresses

Iain Bell   *Heritage Conservation, Planning Division, Essex County Council, Chelmsford CM1 1QH*

Peter Froste   *47 Leys Avenue, Cambridge CB4 2AN*

Frank Gardiner   *23 Beaumont Close, Walton-on-the-Naze, Essex CO14 8TX*

Roger Massey-Ryan *Heritage Conservation, Planning Division, Essex County Council, Chelmsford CM1 1QH*

Nick Nethercoat *Heritage Conservation, Planning Division, Essex County Council, Chelmsford CM1 1QH*

Benjamin Perkins *Park Farm, Liston, Sudbury, Suffolk CO10 7HT*

Alec Wade   *45 Maldon Road, Colchester, Essex CO3 3AQ*

Colour Origination and Printed by ESSEX *Print* & GRAPHICS 01245 398140, part of Essex County Council, from digital media supplied